Clinical Treatment Directions for Infidelity

Clinical Treatment Directions for Infidelity considers the psychotherapeutic treatment of infidelity from a fresh perspective. Psychotherapy (both couples and individual) for infidelity is notoriously challenging, and clinicians tend to disagree on case conceptualizations and treatment objectives. This book approaches infidelity from a client-centered, phenomenological perspective, informed by qualitative research and social context. Essential for clinicians who work with cases of infidelity, it provides a framework and set of tools with which to approach these cases from a non-judgmental stance that helps clients glean meaning from these experiences and make conscious personal choices about how to move forward.

Nicolle Zapien, PhD, is a licensed psychotherapist in private practice in San Francisco, an AASECT certified sex therapist, and the dean of the School of Professional Psychology and Health at the California Institute of Integral Studies. She holds a PhD in psychology from Saybrook University, an MA in counseling psychology from the Professional School of Psychology, and an EdM in teaching and curriculum from Harvard University. She lives in Berkeley, California, with her husband, two children, and beloved rescue dog.

D1596584

Clinical Treatment Directions for Infidelity

A Phenomenological Framework
for Understanding

Nicolle Zapien

Routledge
Taylor & Francis Group
NEW YORK AND LONDON

First published 2018
by Routledge
711 Third Avenue, New York, NY 10017

and by Routledge
2 Park Square, Milton Park, Abingdon, Oxon, OX14 4RN

Routledge is an imprint of the Taylor & Francis Group, an informa business

© 2018 Taylor & Francis

The right of Nicolle Zapien to be identified as author of this work has been asserted by her in accordance with sections 77 and 78 of the Copyright, Designs and Patents Act 1988.

Trademark notice: Product or corporate names may be trademarks or registered trademarks, and are used only for identification and explanation without intent to infringe.

Library of Congress Cataloging-in-Publication Data
Names: Zapien, Nicolle, author.
Title: Clinical treatment directions for infidelity /
    Nicolle Zapien.
Description: New York, NY : Routledge, 2018. | Includes
    bibliographical references.
Identifiers: LCCN 2017042064 (print) | LCCN 2017050743
    (ebook) | ISBN 9781315213118 (eBook) | ISBN
    9780415790482 (hardback) | ISBN 9780415790499 (pbk.)
Subjects: LCSH: Marital psychotherapy. | Adultery.
Classification: LCC RC488.5 (ebook) | LCC RC488.5 .Z37
    2018 (print) | DDC 616.89/1562—dc23
LC record available at https://lccn.loc.gov/2017042064

ISBN: 978-0-415-79048-2 (hbk)
ISBN: 978-0-415-79049-9 (pbk)
ISBN: 978-1-315-21311-8 (ebk)

Typeset in Sabon
by Apex CoVantage, LLC

This book is dedicated to those who have shared their stories of infidelity with me. It is a difficult topic to lay bare for public inquiry and analysis; your bravery has made this book possible. I also dedicate this book to my husband, who has provided me equal doses of levity, freedom, and stability in our marriage.

Contents

Preface

This book is intended for clinicians who treat cases of infidelity. It may also be of interest to other health care providers, married couples, or anyone who is dating because infidelity at this point in history is an entry point into discussions about sexuality and technology, both of which are somewhat universally relevant. It is likely also of interest to anyone who has had an affair, been betrayed, or contemplated either of these possibilities.

In some ways I cannot claim to be an expert on infidelity, sexuality, or technology issues, since my training leading to licensure as a Marriage and Family Therapist (MFT) did not include an emphasis on any of these topics.[1] In 2004, I completed the required courses that precede the 3,000 hours of supervised clinical internship for MFTs in California. These courses included a three-unit course, Couples Dynamics, and a one-unit elective course on human sexuality. I took these courses and the remaining required courses (e.g. Psychological Assessment, Aging and Human Development, Spousal and Child Abuse, Alcohol and Chemical Dependency, Ethical Practice, Psychopharmacology, Family Systems, and Counseling Techniques) in preparation for licensure to treat clients who had marital concerns, including infidelity, among a broad range of other issues.

At the same time I was starting as a clinician in 2004, a seismic economic and cultural change was taking place. It was the same year that Facebook and OkCupid were founded, and three years before the first iPhone came to market. At that time, Blackberrys and Nokia brand Personal Data Assistants (PDAs) dominated the mobile technology market in the United States (US). Many people were beginning to use them to make calls, send and receive email, and text message more frequently largely because of their portability and convenience. Dating and hook-up sites, such as Match.com, eHarmony, and Gay.com, among others, had already been in existence for many years by then. Online porn was in a generative phase as an industry, growing at exponential rates as computing processing speeds and Internet infrastructure developed. In

2004, PDAs were not particularly "smart" compared to today's devices. Searching websites that featured audio, images, and video, which were and still are prominent on dating, hook-up, and porn sites, took place on desktop computers at home (and for some people also at work) at that time. It was after the advent of the iPhone—coupled with ever more powerful and fast personal computing capabilities—that many more dating, hook-up, and porn sites targeting every imaginable sub-segment of the population and sexual interest would emerge and be used on the go, more frequently and by an increasing number of people.

Since 2004, I completed my clinical internships and launched a private psychotherapy practice in downtown San Francisco. I figured it would be a good idea to locate my office close to public transportation so that my clients could easily come to therapy before or after work or during lunch breaks. I chose the historic Flood Building, near the shopping district on the edge of the financial district with a small office and waiting room. What I didn't anticipate at that time was that the influence of Silicon Valley and the impacts of disruptive technology and their sequelae would soon be felt very strongly in downtown San Francisco. Cranes began to populate the skyline and developers built high rises at a record pace. Many start-ups and tech companies soon moved into the neighborhood and fancy renovation and redesign projects abounded. The increased traffic, steep rise in rents, and acute crisis of increased homelessness became palpable in the neighborhood. In the time I have been a psychotherapist with my office in this location, San Francisco has been shaped by tremendous growth and innovation. These changes have also driven what appear to be significant social and emotional changes in its people in a very short time period.

These changes were not only apparent to me through my own observations but were also echoed in the stories that clients discussed in psychotherapy sessions. In fact, these changes were palpable even before the therapy began, in the ways they used technology to make appointments, traveled to and entered the office space, and related to the psychotherapeutic endeavor itself. What I have noticed over the years is that more and more clients come to session still using their devices or feel compelled to check them intermittently during session.

They also now describe relational issues and conflicts that transpire entirely via Facebook or Instagram, or through dating apps, hook-up apps, chat, or text message. Some of them have had relationships that exist solely within these media including sexual and romantic ones where they have never met the other person face to face. These relationships develop largely without the guidance of facial cues or tone of voice, but instead through a different set of social behaviors (e.g. reply all, bcc, capitalizations, emoticons, ghosting, benching, zombieing). Clients also began to marvel at the ways they might access like-minded people and affinity groups and feel connected to others immediately through technology in ways unprecedented in history. Flirting or communicating with others separately from one's spouse or partner via technology occurred more frequently. Some found evidence of an affair or a betrayal through digital pictures, email, or texts. And many learned about sexuality through porn or online dating apps if they consumed these media. Some even began to question whether they had Internet, porn, or dating app addictions. Others reasoned that when relationships got difficult, all they had to do was select their app of choice to find new relationships that they surmised would meet their needs rather than work through issues in relationships or therapy.

The changes since 2004 were significant, yet my training, as noted earlier, did not include much discussion of sexuality, hook-ups, open relationships, or infidelity, but it included even *less* discussion of the potential impact of technology on relationships or sexuality. The majority of academic and clinical research, and relevant psychological theorizing about infidelity for clinical application in the US, for example, had largely occurred before the current historical context that includes technology's impact on our relationships and sexual experiences. It seemed only fitting therefore to consider infidelity anew against the backdrop of contemporary phenomena in context. With this focus, it is not my intent to take a position of hand-wringing with respect to technological advances or sexual behavior in this book. There is potentially a need, however, for consideration of technoethics and improved collective sexual literacy to support our understanding of both realms. In this book, I aim simply to refresh the clinical view of infidelity for the times.

My interest in infidelity specifically, from among the many other potentially interesting relational phenomena that are occurring at this point in history, arose largely out of several clinical cases that presented in my practice in the last decade. These were cases of clients who were either having affairs, contemplating having affairs, or dealing with the aftermath of infidelity in the very particular place and time described earlier. In working with these clients, I began to consider how the ways I had been trained to conceptualize such experiences would lead me to consider infidelity as a relational trauma, an attachment issue, in terms of object-relations theories or family systems dynamics. Guided by this training, I assessed for individual psychopathology that might be beneath the infidelity, and I began to consider the relational and attachment histories of the couple. All of the treatment plans devised in these cases were usually somewhat effective and helpful to clients. Somehow, however, these views of approaching infidelity seemed to fall short because they largely ignored both the sexual issues and the role of technology in the infidelities, which were so prescient. In addition, many of these cases didn't squarely fit into any of the diagnostic categories or theoretical ideas. The sheer number of these cases caused me to question whether or not an increase in infidelity was occurring, as I hadn't (at that time anyway) advertised infidelity as a specialty of mine. I also wondered, if there was indeed an increase, if it might be related to larger sociological phenomena and thus may not be a result of an individually experienced pathology or a particular couple's dynamic and therefore if it warranted a shift in our collective clinical views. What followed were three different, but related, research projects and a dissertation undertaken in 2013 and 2014 on the phenomenon of infidelity from the perspective of the person who begins an affair.

What I didn't understand at the time was how evocative infidelity is for many people. This became apparent after announcing my desire to study this particular issue to my future dissertation committee. They promptly asked a great number of questions about my intentions and about the implications of my future research. Was I implicitly or explicitly wishing to defend or justify the actions of those who cheated? Did I wish to align my thinking with any particular clinical approach or psychological theories? What was problematic specifically with the current ways infidelity is theorized and treated? Did I hold any particular views about marriage, monogamy, polyamory, or sexuality that may influence the findings? Did I hope to find the cause of infidelity? Did I think there was a cause? And if so, was there an implied intent, therefore, to prevent affairs? Did I think that people chose consciously to have affairs, or were they perhaps a drive, an unconscious process, or something else? The questions continued. What was my personal relationship to the topic? Why did I wish to focus my interests on those who cheat and not the couple or the one who is betrayed or the other person or persons in the triangle? Would it be interesting or illustrative to consider the views of all of them? What makes the current ubiquitous personal and portable technology use in the US uniquely different as a context for infidelity? What is timeless and essential about the experience, if anything? And how would my research offer new insight to the many ways that infidelity is already understood in the literature and is treated clinically?

At that time, I hadn't yet fully understood that to study infidelity demanded that I consider how it has been largely conflated in the literature and in society with unquestioned beliefs, values, and judgments that differ significantly from person to person, a fact that would benefit from consideration separately from the issue itself. I also didn't understand just how personally, historically, and culturally situated the meaning of infidelity in general or in a particular affair might be. It became clear from these early questions, reading the literature, personal reflections, and every subsequent personal and professional discussion of the issue that in order to investigate and contribute something novel to the literature that could be used by clinicians to improve clinical conceptualizations in cases of infidelity, I would need to question the meaning and implications of my findings from a philosophical perspective. It was also clear that there would be multiple theoretical perspectives to consider as explanatory of the issue and that each of these could likely be justified—all of them could also be questioned. One goal for this project, therefore, was to strip away these layers and to consider the phenomenon in a descriptive manner, as separate and distinct from the theorizing or valuing processes. I hoped that through such an endeavor, something new would become apparent about the experience of infidelity that would inform a new clinical perspective.

At the same time, I want to be clear to the reader that I am not taking this descriptive stance because I wish to provide an analysis that is valueless and atheoretical and wash my hands (and help those who have affairs wash theirs) of taking responsibility on the issue. My goal is not to defend infidelity. I have been privy to a great number of clinical examples and personal stories from friends and family, which illustrate how painful and destructive infidelity can be for all involved. It is rare with hindsight that people are proud of infidelities and much more common that they feel regretful. Betrayal is not a pro-social behavior, and the potential negative consequences to the one who is betrayed and any other family members who are affected can be profound and long lasting. More often than not, when a partner discovers an affair, conflict and divorce follow. If kept secret, often (but not always), intimacy suffers and shame festers. Children, if there are any, can be impacted in terms of difficulties with trust and their future perceptions of relationships (Lusterman, 2005a). Yet at the same time, the oversimplification of discussions of infidelity as wholly negative and hurtful forecloses inquiry too soon for all involved about the larger issues of desire, freedom, eroticism, and inflexible perceptions of the partner that are often beneath and embedded within instances of infidelity. Such a perspective also implicitly privileges monogamy and fails to make space for explorations of other relationship structures, which for some people are entirely workable, valid, and preferred. Offering a non-pathological, non-moralizing, descriptive view of how we come to make meaning of marriage, commitment, sexuality, and desires that individuals and couples face through infidelity is another aim of this work. It is not a pro-marriage, pro-monogamy, pro-infidelity, or a pro–open relationships book. Instead it is an invitation to enter a series of deeper questions that instances of infidelity afford us.

In addition, for clinicians who still receive so little training in sexuality and technologically mediated relationships, the hope is that this book will provide direction for thoughtful approaches to psychotherapy that fills some of the gaps in our training. Because clinicians have been found to disagree widely on case conceptualizations of infidelity and also seem to align their treatment goals with their own experiences with marriage, divorce, non-monogamy, infidelity, and feelings about each rather than what might be clinically useful to the clients themselves, another aim is to provide relevant and client-centered treatment directions that help to eradicate these potential biases and issues.

I have organized the chapters in this book as follows. We begin with a discussion of the issues associated with defining infidelity in chapter 1 and consider the recent historical background of the concept. This is followed by a review of the prevalence of this difficult-to-define phenomenon and some descriptive statistics from the literature on infidelity as well as a critique of the methods used to study infidelity, presented in chapter 2. Psychotherapeutic approaches to infidelity and the ways that these approaches may be limiting or biased for psychotherapists who treat infidelity and their clients are presented in chapter 3. In chapter 4, I discuss phenomenological research as a means to facilitate understanding of the phenomenon in a more essential manner as separate and distinct from the processes of valuing, judging, and theorizing about infidelity. This method was used to gather the data for three different studies of infidelity, which are summarized in chapter 5. These data are also considered together with evidence from clinical cases, as well as hypothetical instances. In all cases, examples, and illustrations, permission has been granted to use the stories, and the information has been disguised to protect the anonymity of the sources. However, the details that are relevant to the discussion have been preserved. These narratives and their analysis inform a novel clinical conceptualization and treatment directions for infidelity, discussed in chapter 6. Chapter 7 offers a series of exercises that you can do to build your own capacity to understand and support clients more effectively. It is my hope that the reader finds these chapters thought-provoking, helpful, and practical to use right away in clinical work. I also hope that this discussion helps us all to strengthen and deepen our awareness and empathic skills in our own most important relationships.

Acknowledgments

First and foremost I want to thank my husband, children, and friends for being patient and encouraging throughout this process. I wrote this book, for the most part, while they were at work and school. However, with a full-time faculty position and a part-time clinical practice, squeezing in writing necessitated some sacrifices and required tight scheduling. As a result, I had less energy and free time for fun or restorative activities, and this likely had some impact on all of my relationships. Throughout this process, however, my loved ones were confident in my abilities and supportive of my book and were poised to celebrate its completion and my reentry into the usual activities. For this I am thankful.

I wish to thank the California Institute of Integral Studies, and in particular Drs. Judie Wexler, Meg Jordan, and Michelle Marzullo, who recognized the importance of supporting my scholarship and writing by protecting my time through partial course release programs not always granted for projects such as this but very much appreciated in this case. I am grateful for their support.

I am deeply appreciative of my clients and the participants in the various research endeavors who have provided their stories of infidelity for use in this book. Because this topic is often fraught with shame and is a subject of much judgment by others, it is the brave individual who shares these details with another, particularly when they will be analyzed and discussed in this format. I am hopeful that this book will be used to develop skillful ways of addressing the many concerns and feelings that infidelity so often evokes in service of helping others.

It is important to give particular mention here to the key researchers and thinkers upon whose shoulders I stand. Shirley Glass, Amadeo Giorgi, Kathrine Hertlein, Esther Perel, and Fred Piercy, in particular, as well as a great number or scholars and theorists, have influenced my work. It is not easy to study and write about infidelity without being brave, and I recognize that researching this topic beginning in 2013 is easier for me because of your earlier contributions. Your thinking has paved the way for mine, and while we may not agree on all points, I deeply respect that which has come before me.

I also wish to thank Dr. Gina Ogden for putting me in touch with the editors at Routledge who encouraged me to publish my findings in this format. Her warmth and generosity in supporting up and coming generations of researchers and clinicians is threaded throughout her long and illustrious career and has been incredibly helpful to me at this stage of mine. It has been tremendous to be counted among her mentees, and I have learned many things large and small from her and from her example.

I want to thank Elizabeth Graber and George Zimmar, editors at Routledge, for seeing the value in my work and supporting me smoothly through the process of publication and for being so easy to work with.

To Nora Isaacs, a dear friend of mine, and gifted professional writer, who volunteered to read the manuscript pre-submission and offered valuable suggestions and insightful feedback. Because I have only ever written a dissertation and a handful of academic articles, Nora helped to provide coaching about writing a book and was a champion and cheerleader throughout. I am greatly indebted to her contribution to this work.

And to Nicolas Ferlatte, another dear friend, who shares my love of philosophy and with whom I have had many conversations about various aspects of this project. Nicolas has always demonstrated tremendous flexibility of thinking and insight in these dialogues, and I am grateful for his contributions to this manuscript, his warmth, and his friendship.

I also engaged my long-time friend, Ruth Greenberg, who is among the most gifted couples therapists I know and a writer in her own right, to read the manuscript before submission. Her encouragement for me to show up and put myself out there has been important to my developing sense of courage in this endeavor and throughout my life. And her friendship is more important to me than I can describe.

Note

1 The dearth in training on sexuality and infidelity is not unique to MFTs and is equally absent in the required training of social workers, licensed professional clinical counselors, and licensed clinical psychologists. Psychiatrists receive the requisite anatomy and physiology of sexuality as part of their medical training, and psychoanalysts are well prepared to address the psychoanalytic aspects of sexuality and desire from within the psychoanalytic framework but are largely not prepared to address many other aspects of sexuality.

Part I

Chapter 1

What Is Infidelity?

I asked him what monogamy really means in practice in our marriage. He found the question confusing at first, and stated simply, that he knows and I know and that it's difficult to be concrete, but what constitutes a breach should be clear to both of us by now. He seemed annoyed by the discussion. When pushed further, he noted that everyone thinks about other people in a sexual way but if those thoughts are more detailed and go on for more than 5 minutes or so, then this is what begins an affair or at the very least is the beginning of a significant problem. For him the mastery of his mind is what makes monogamy possible. I have a very creative mind that wanders in a great number of directions everyday, including fantasies and fears about all aspects of life some of which last more than 5 minutes. For me fidelity includes not acting on these ideas, or at least not more than what I call "harmless flirting." Apparently, we do not agree on what monogamy or infidelity is in practice.

—Anonymous

Infidelity is difficult to define concretely in that its meaning is not univocal or intersubjectively agreed upon (Cossman, 2006). Historically, infidelity was a term used to describe someone who is unfaithful, doubtful, or a non-believer in a religious sense. In this century in the US the term has been most frequently used to describe a breach in monogamous sexual behavior for couples, particularly married couples. There are many other terms that are related to infidelity that have also been used in this century, but they have largely fallen out of fashion due to their lack of applicability to various types of relationships that are gaining more acceptance, or because they are overly specific in terms of the ways in which such betrayals might occur. Some examples include: Extra-marital sex; extra-marital affairs; extra-dyadic sex; two-timing; adultery; having a fling or an affair; cuckoldry; and cheating, to name a few.

For most of this book, I will use the term *infidelity*, defined as an act or acts of betrayal of a sexual and/or emotionally intimate nature *as*

perceived by one or both parties of a couple (Glass, 2003). This definition of infidelity places perceptions at its center and these perceptions can
be said to be a product of both individual factors and contextual factors
that are filtered through culturally and historically situated meanings.
At particular times, however, I may also use the term *affair* to describe
particular acts or instances of infidelity. This is also consistent with the
most-used terms in my recent clinical cases and among research participants in the studies conducted that inform this book.

I am choosing the term infidelity and this particular definition from
among others, because it allows for inclusion of many types of betrayals. For example, infidelity includes betrayals within various relationship structures such as marriages, domestic partnerships, other types of
pairings, poly structures, and open relationships as long as a betrayal is
perceived by at least one person involved.[1] Infidelity with this definition
also does not require a perceived betrayal through embodied or physical contact, and may include a betrayal that occurs through technology-
mediated contact, for example. This is a relatively new phenomenon in
an historical sense, but one that is nevertheless occurring more and more
frequently (Young, 2008).[2] The term infidelity, which may be the most
fitting for contemporary experiences and is most inclusive from among
the other options, is therefore referring to a wider range of different acts
and experiences than ever before.

Before we delve into the research on infidelity in the next chapters, it
is important to mention some historical roots of infidelity and how these
may influence our perceptions or views. Infidelity, referred to historically
as adultery, has its roots in many of the major religious texts.[3] I will not
diverge to explore these texts here, nor will I discuss how adultery is
treated in each text except to say that the arguments against adultery in
these texts are moral ones. As a whole, these arguments tend to caution
believers not to be tempted by selfish desires—in particular desires and
impulses originating in the body—in order to remain faithful to a higher
religious or spiritual purpose. Within these moral arguments against
desire, there is often a discussion of the problematic nature of immoral
adulterous thoughts as well as immoral adulterous acts. The general idea
is that immoral thoughts lead us through temptation to immoral acts—
the urges that reside in the body are not to be trusted when thoughts are
impure.

Adultery, as it has been defined in the legal lexicon, has historically
also been punishable by law (Cossman, 2006). In legal cases in recent
history in the US, adultery was defined as extra-marital penetrative penis-
vagina intercourse, which was illegal for both men and women to engage
in outside of their marriages, although the law was not applied equally
to men in such cases. The reasoning for this discrepancy related to a
lack of availability of reliable birth control until 1972, the lack of access

to safe abortions before 1973[4] in the US, and the concern that women who strayed would conceive children who were not from the betrayed husband's seed and that he would be nevertheless obligated to care for.[5] From the perspective of the law, marriage is both a financial and a legal contract. In cases of adultery, bastard children, to use another historical term, represented a breach of this contract and an unfair financial burden to the betrayed husband. Over time, advances in birth control, changes in child custody and divorce laws, and women's rights, as well as some very evocative legal trials of adultery cases, have caused the courts to question the need for legal involvement in cases of adultery altogether. The pivotal case to highlight this shift occurred in 1987, when a woman was charged with adultery after her husband found her having masturbated another man (Cossman, 2006).[6] This was among the first of many cases that shifted the focus away from intercourse and the possibility of pregnancy and instead moved toward defining adultery by the *subjective feelings of betrayal* on the part of the betrayed spouse. This led to the idea that any type of betrayal of trust of the spouse with anyone else, regardless of gender, or even without physical contact, could be considered adulterous if it were perceived as a betrayal. This, coupled with the addition of no-fault divorce laws in some states and the pervasiveness of infidelity, has largely catapulted these types of cases out of courtrooms and relegated them to personal relational disputes to be addressed in private or through couples counseling. The only exception is divorce and child custody decisions in states that do not have no-fault divorce laws. In these states, perceived adultery can be used as evidence in expediting divorce decisions and in influencing child custody decisions to the detriment of whomever is perceived to have committed adultery.

What remains central to the definition of infidelity today is *perception*. This is interesting because perceptions vary between people, can be said to depend on a great number of variables, and can change over time. For example, to consider what constitutes a perceived infidelity to any particular individual at any particular point in time refers back to the original promise and understanding of fidelity in the past, which is also a perceptual (and a memory and a socio-linguistic) exercise. While we may agree that there was a promise of fidelity at a particular point in time, what each of the participants understood concretely at that time is a perception that may not be shared or may not hold the exact same meaning to each in an ongoing manner.

While it may be clear to most, for example, that ongoing intercourse with another person outside of a couple constitutes a betrayal in sexually monogamous relationships, the limits of the types of interactions that one can have with others outside of a monogamous relationship that are less clear are often not discussed in detail as one makes the original promise of fidelity. It is within these interactions that the seeds of infidelities often begin. Couples who subscribe to the same moral or religious ideas often have a clearer idea of what constitutes fidelity, sometimes guided by religious practices and doctrines, and often are more granular about prohibited types of interactions. Even so there are many possible interactions that can remain potentially unclear. Further, even if they are articulated in detail, we have all had disagreements with someone that involve different perceptions of the same situation. This will be explored in more detail in chapter 5 through research participant narratives, but at this juncture I offer one such example from a study of a participant describing how his perception and his wife's perceptions of what constitutes a betrayal differed and also how they changed over time:

> This lady walked in . . . and this was in the late spring or early summer and she walked in lightly dressed and barefoot because she had been gardening and she lived around the corner and so I was pretty struck with her immediately, so that's how we actually met and then . . . (sigh) . . . there were various kinds of socializing things and I found myself very attracted to her quickly and I proceeded to be friendly with her. So we established a sort of relationship although it was not physical, in fact it wasn't physical or sexual until much later, in fact after, um, my wife at the time and I had split up. I don't think I considered it an affair and I know she didn't at the time. My wife knew it was an affair. It was certainly a mess.

In this case, he describes feelings of attraction and socializing with another woman and the establishment of a "sort of relationship." His wife perceived this as an affair at the time even though he did not. He later comes to have a sexual and intimate relationship with this woman after he breaks up with his wife. We can easily understand the wife in her perceptions, particularly given that we know that he eventually did have a sexual relationship with the other woman after the break-up and that she intuited this all along. We can assume that the wife perceived something that he did not wish to acknowledge but was nevertheless somehow present to her before they divorced. It is also possible, however, that his perception is more fitting or is potentially equally valid. He was attracted to the other woman but did not engage physically or sexually with her while committed to his wife; thus he upheld his commitment to her, technically. Regardless of how each of us might judge the characters in this story, many of us find ourselves attracted to any number of people we might meet without intending to become attracted to them at the outset. And in these cases, how we navigate the feelings of attraction is what differentiates instances of infidelity from fleeting attractions. In the description, however, the man and his wife have different perceptions of the moment that the line is crossed and the affair has come to be. Regardless of which views an outsider takes, of whether or not this was a betrayal and whatever the line might be over which he may have crossed, it is not something they agreed upon at the same moment in time.

Another issue related to perception is defining what constitutes a *sexual*, *erotic*, or *intimate* moment. While each of us can perceive and name an interaction to be flirtatious, erotic, or intimate, it is also possible that the person we engage with or some outside viewer may have different perceptions of the meaning of the event. Merleau-Ponty (2012), a phenomenologist who wrote extensively on perception and sexuality, defines all sexuality as the body-subject's concrete, spatial, and pre-reflective intentionality or directedness toward the lived world. What is most interesting for the current discussion is the *pre-reflective* and *embodied* quality of sexual intentionality that he describes. He states, "Insofar as I have hands, feet, a body, I sustain around me intentions which are not dependent on my decisions and which affect my surroundings in a way that I do not choose. This isn't accomplished through will or intellectualization but through conversations or gesture" (Merleau-Ponty, 2012, p. 440). Merleau-Ponty essentially suggests that what is sexual may not be available to us in a conscious and reflective manner in the form of a decision or a cognitive process but is present instead in our embodied manner. This becomes sometimes available later to consciousness to be named erotic, sexual, or intimate and reflected upon, but other times remains unavailable to consciousness and therefore not reflected upon or named as such. Most clinicians would agree that we each have varying degrees of conscious awareness of our feelings, sensations, and desires at any given point in time and further that sometimes even when aware we may be reluctant to acknowledge them. In addition, clinicians also would likely agree that we differ in our ability to read somatic cues and gestures of others and to discern intended (or subconscious) meaning of embodied acts in real time. These two ideas are prevalent in many psychological theories and should come as no surprise asserted here, and yet when applied to the issue of infidelity, unconscious or pre-conscious embodied processes will become important in our understanding and treatment directions in some novel ways.

It may be helpful to provide an illustration here about how eroticism and sexuality can be experienced in a pre-conscious embodied manner. In my clinical work as a psychotherapist and sex therapist, I find that many sexually monogamous married couples opt for the "usual" arrangement, which does not include sexual intercourse with another outside of the relationship. This is supported by the cultural hegemony. This arrangement goes largely unquestioned and largely unarticulated because it is seen as synonymous with the institution of marriage, even if the couple is not religious. In addition, for most couples there is some degree of clarity (although not always) and agreement, either verbally or otherwise understood, about other boundaries such as permissible types of touch with others, for example. Often the line is drawn at hugging and kissing in a socially acceptable manner (e.g. on the cheek among close friends) but not "making out" or passionate tongue kissing. There is some variance on the particulars of this line based on differences in cultural norms and personalities and beliefs about the role of kissing, hugging, and touching in social situations and couples relationships, but the line is generally somewhat clear to couples and defines the distinction between social touch and sexual touch, even if it has not been discussed. This line is learned and communicated socially through gesture and embodied interactions or conversations that occur over time. Some rare few discuss in greater detail their views and ideas about monogamy and sexuality and make agreements to open their marriages in particular ways through swinging, cuddle parties, cuckoldry, or allowing making out or other specific activities that are generally more sexual, sensual, or erotic than what can be described as socially acceptable touch in a broad non-sexual manner.

There is still a gray area, however. Some touches or gestures that are understood as more broadly socially acceptable can be imbued with a sexual atmosphere or intimate sensibility. Take such circumstances like a pat on the back, an embrace through partner dance, or a handshake—all of which might be socially sanctioned and somewhat innocuous to an outside observer. Such touches can also be very intimate, erotic, or sexual as experienced by those who are involved in them and sometimes in an unanticipated manner. In addition, a wide array of social possibilities that one might encounter that do not include touching but nevertheless can be said to be sexual or intimate exist, such as flirting, making or receiving sexually suggestive comments, divulging or receiving intimate thoughts and secrets from another, or fantasizing about another during sex with the primary partner. These experiences of eroticism and intimacy (or if unwanted, harassment) can be pre-meditated insofar as one can call up a fantasy at will or consciously try to flirt. But these examples can, as Merleau-Ponty suggests, also occur in ways that are not always consciously available to us until *after they are already occurring and are named or labeled erotic or intimate*. Similarly, situations such as having dinner with an attractive colleague while on a business trip or wearing a sexy outfit to a public event may all be socially sanctioned or defensible within the structure of monogamous relationships, particularly if we intend to remain neutral or boundaried in sexual acts with others. Each of these situations as well as a great number of others are contexts where eroticism may become present in an embodied pre-reflective manner within these acts and then represent areas of gray.

We all have opinions and judgments about each of the scenarios discussed earlier, ranging from nonchalance to clear discomfort. Depending on a wide range of contextual details and meanings for all involved (e.g. who the other is, how we judge their character, how connected we feel to our spouse, how insecure we feel, our attachment style), any of these or all of these situations could be perceived as a betrayal or not. Often these distinctions are not made upfront but instead only get discussed once one of these scenarios has occurred and a threat is perceived or if the experience develops into something more than anticipated for the person experiencing it. What is interesting about these distinctions is that while we may be able to sort out where to draw the line on one of these issues or all of them that we may brainstorm in advance, we are usually unable to fully anticipate all future possible scenarios, contexts, feelings, and experiences that may occur, in advance, and until death or the primary relationship ends. There is an ongoing stream of new experiences and contexts that may also be in a gray area or may give rise to a new set of feelings, desires, or subjective understandings of the boundaries between fidelity and infidelity.

Take a moment to consider what for you personally would constitute infidelity so that you can become more aware of your beliefs and values. If you are a clinician, this is an important activity so that you might become more aware and flexible with your consciousness as you approach clinical work in service of your clients. Consider what for you would seem fitting as the definition of infidelity? Where for you are the lines? Are there gray areas? What are the agreements you have within your relationship(s) (if you are currently in any) about fidelity? Are you clear and in agreement with your partner(s)? Have you discussed this? What would it be like to discuss this? What are the risks and benefits of doing so?

The Difficulties With Defining Infidelity and Studying Infidelity

It is not only the perceptions and judgment of the persons engaging in the potential infidelity that are relevant. Perceived social judgment is also relevant. For example, in research on infidelity, non-response bias and social desirability biases are prevalent and demonstrate that not only are the perceptions that people have about infidelity varied, but that often they are difficult to capture. Responses to research, when provided, are often distorted to match social mores when they are discussed.

One salient example occurred in response to the call for participants for one of my studies on infidelity, which appears below.

Dear Colleagues and Friends,

I am a PhD candidate at Saybrook University, an accredited research institution in San Francisco, studying psychology. I am also a licensed and practicing MFT in San Francisco who works with both couples and individuals. Currently, I am working on my dissertation research—an exploration of the experiences of adults who have had an extra-marital affair. Ultimately, the hope is that the results will provide information about how people experience these situations and will inform improved clinical interventions so that we might support our clients better.

If you know of an adult who has been married for five years or more who may have had an affair, I would welcome the referral to the study.

Participation will include a short telephone call to outline the parameters of the study, gather consent, and answer any questions and then each participant will be interviewed via phone at a time of mutual convenience for an hour. All responses will be reported confidentially and anonymously. If you would like to recommend someone for participation please have him or her call me or email me. Thank you so much in advance for your help.

Best,
Nicolle Zapien

Upon announcing that I was interested in gathering narratives describing the experience for those beginning an affair, not very many people were interested in participating. I expected this. Research on sexual behavior or other relatively private topics often presents a challenge in garnering participation (Dunn et al., 1997; Catania, Gibson, Chitwood, & Coates, 1990). Potential participants have to feel trust in the researcher and yet at the same time need to feel anonymity. They further need to understand and value the purpose of the project in order to see that it is worthwhile to put their personal relational and sexual secrets in public view (Farkas, Sine, & Evans, 1978; Plaud, Gaither, Hegstad, Rowan, & Devitt, 1999; Marcus & Schütz, 2005). These issues are difficult to balance in recruiting. Usually with difficult recruiting endeavors for research such as this one, there is a lack of response altogether—people ignore the call for participants and simply do not take the time to respond at all. If they do, they send curt replies indicating that they are unwilling. In this particular study, however, this was not the case.

Several people instead responded with relatively lengthy narratives describing their infidelities, fantasies, and regrets but also described why they didn't want to participate in the research study or sign the consent form. These non-responders (those who have not formally consented to participate in the study), offered insight into the forces that come to bear on non-response biases in data collection endeavors on infidelity, in addition to illuminating what was potentially missing in the data set from the responders (those who did formally consent to participate and responded to the interview questions) through their stories. Non-response responders often sent their reply from their personal email addresses, thus revealing who they were to the researcher and some of the details of the affairs. But without consent to use their responses, they could not be used for analysis.

This partial reveal of their affairs but also lack of willingness to participate in the study was very interesting. I wanted permission to analyze their non-response responses too. I consulted with the Institutional Review Board (IRB) at the California Institute of Integral Studies, the group that evaluates research ethics for human subjects. They granted me permission to re-contact these people who had already sent me a response but declined participation in the study and ask them to fill out a consent form to use their original comments already received via email for a paper about non-response bias and social desirability in sexuality research.

These emails revealed a range of reasons for non-participation and a host of issues that underpin the phenomenon that otherwise would not necessarily have been apparent from the data collected from consenting participants in the study itself. For example, even though my call for participants stated that I was seeking participants who had had an affair, some responded to describe, in detail complete with much grief and upset, how they themselves had been betrayed. These people often, after describing the hurtful events, offered their former spouse's name and contact information and in some cases asked if I would recruit them for the study directly. (Of course, I didn't, as this would not be ethical.) These people clearly did not misunderstand the target participant criteria, as they offered the name of someone they thought I should recruit who would meet the criteria. At the same time they wanted me to have their side of the story as someone who had been betrayed, complete with all the grief and pain, ostensibly to counterbalance what they anticipated I might hear from those who had an affair. They also didn't want to forward the call for participants to their exes themselves. Their suggestion to have me contact their former spouses was also accompanied by a quip about how participation in the study might help the spouse to get help through reflecting upon his or her actions.

Others sent an email reply that suggested that they had had an affair but also preferred to keep the details secret. The fact that they replied, revealing their email address and name to me, is not entirely secretive and is therefore somewhat paradoxical and intriguing. These emails were usually witty, coy, and, one could argue, even flirty and playful. They were like short riddles in a way. I got a glimpse into a partial reveal of the experience and the atmosphere of play and witty banter that sexuality sometimes includes. They also demonstrated a view into the compartmentalized or split aspects of the self in infidelity situations. These people were both prideful and boastful and also secretive but not entirely so. I could sense their desire for me to play a role opposite them with either a playful and witty retort or a scolding response. Because engaging in either manner would have been unethical and inappropriate, I did not respond to the content of these types of emails other than to ask if they wanted to participate formally in the research project, ask them to sign an attached consent form, and offer to discuss any questions they may have. In these cases, I inevitably received no reply. These types of responses were among the most fascinating—if they truly wanted their secrets to remain hidden, they could have not replied at all. This particular type of reply suggests that perhaps there are more affairs than are documented in the prevalence rates in the literature and that perhaps there are particular aspects of compartmentalization of shame and pride that make it challenging for affairs to be understood fully in an integrated manner by researchers, clinicians, and people experiencing them.

The non-response responses came in other forms. Some divulged that they wished they had had an affair and described a missed opportunity for one or fantasies about having an affair either in general or with a specific person or people. Others said that they had experienced scenarios that were in a gray area because their spouse or partner had a different view, and they wanted to know if these experiences were relevant for the study. These two groups of scenarios included justifications of flirting or a wish for more freedom than they knew their spouses and partners wanted for them. These non-responders described a variety of activities. Consuming porn in secret, online chatting, viewing dating apps, having friendships with members of the opposite sex, kissing and hugging others, fantasizing about others, making out with others, dancing with others, having a crush on a coworker or neighbor, or flirting in a technologically mediated manner were among them. Because these people didn't see these experiences as acts of infidelity, but their spouses did, and the study required a perception of infidelity for the one experiencing, they were not qualified to participate in the study. This group of responses made clear, however, that a gray area existed and people within a couple did not always agree as to what constitutes infidelity. These responses also made clear that some yearned to explore their fantasies or their desires, despite the reactions they imagined they would get from their partners and society.

The important point about all of these responses is that people took the time to send an email, divulging their identities; describing an aspect of their experiences with the issue; revealing hurt, pride, fantasies, or difficulties with intersubjective agreement on the issue, but they also did not want to fill out the consent form and provide a description of their experiences in full. Many of them, more than in any study so far that I have conducted, wanted to reveal something about the issue but also did not want to formally participate and fully reveal their experiences and have them included in research. While I cannot analyze demographics or other variables of these non-participants who responded to tell me that they didn't want to participate (I didn't technically collect data on them although I did garner consent to analyze their emails to me) they were alluding to the extent to which there is a complex set of social and personal issues that prevents people from full participation and honesty in such studies (and maybe even altogether). And there is no way to know if those who *do* participate in these types of studies are somehow fundamentally different demographically, personality-wise, or in other ways than others.

It follows from these non-response responses that shame, pride, and secrecy are intertwined with infidelity and that there are more cases of infidelity than are counted in research due to non-response biases revealed in the comments. Further, we can assume that among those who participate in research on the topic, they are sharing potentially slightly distorted versions of the experience filtered through their feelings of shame, pride, and secrecy, which we can assume may be present for them as well but perhaps to a lesser extent than those who are non-responders. Social desirability biases, as these distortions are termed, have been noted on studies of sexual behavior (Meston, Heiman, Trapnell, & Paulhus, 1998). In addition, as Merleau-Ponty (2012) pointed out, not all of what people experience as sexual intentionality is always made conscious to the subject. What we ultimately receive as responses then in research studies on infidelity is a discussion of that which is perceived as acceptable to the person to discuss among those who are willing to discuss it and, from that, which is made available to the consciousness of the person offering it to the researcher and which is subjectively defined as infidelity at the time of reporting. The remaining elements, which we can only surmise also exist, remain hidden and unavailable to empirical researchers. This same phenomenon is also likely at play in psychotherapy in that some clients do not reveal to us their infidelities because they do not consider them to be infidelities or do not wish to reveal them fully to us because they deem them socially objectionable. Those who do disclose affairs likely only reveal that which they feel is acceptable to reveal. It is the skillful clinician who can support clients through these layers of experience. And regardless of what the idealized "truth" may be, what we know about infidelity can be ultimately understood as both a hiding and an allowing of desire for someone outside of the primary relationship in different measures, at the same time. With all of this complexity in defining infidelity and researching infidelity, the chapter that follows delves into a brief summary of what is known from within the psychological literature about affairs and infidelity, which has been gathered from peer-reviewed published studies using a wider range of different definitions of the phenomenon, through the lens of social desirability biases, and with significant non-response bias. With these studies, as problematic as they may be, we begin situating the phenomenon against the backdrop of what is known about infidelity.

Notes

1 Within open and poly structures, betrayals and infidelities do occur but often include a perceived betrayal through non-adherence to an agreed-upon limit or protocol that has been established as part of the open structure.
2 From among the many types of betrayals that can occur, there is the least agreement about whether or not technology-mediated relationships constitute a betrayal or an instance of infidelity. Some feel very strongly about porn, Internet chatting, and online friendships and view these as infidelities. Others see these as not problematic at all. This lack of agreement, which is often not discussed at the time a commitment to monogamy is made, provides a fertile context for conflicts and issues to arise (Young, 2008; Braun-Harvey & Vigorito, 2016).
3 Christianity, Hinduism, Islam, and Judaism, some of the most prominent religions in the world, clearly take the position that sexual infidelity is problematic. Buddhism is somewhat less clear, in that the focus in Buddhist texts is sometimes on compassion, dialogue with the spouse, self-compassion, and restraint rather than strict moral judgment of infidelity.
4 Eisenstadt v. Baird made contraception available to unmarried persons in 1972; Roe v. Wade in 1973 made safe and legal abortions available to women. These two cases combined afforded women the possibility to plan pregnancies and act more autonomously in sexual relationships in the US.
5 In addition to the right to vote and the various contraception cases that offered women in the US more freedom and control over family planning, there were numerous cases that have supported women's rights to work, women's rights to equal pay and to non-discrimination based on sex (e.g. Phillips v. Martin Marietta Corp, 1971; Reed v. Reed, 1971; International Union v. Johnson Controls Inc.) in the early 1970s. These cases have supported transformations in how marriage, divorce, sex, and infidelity are viewed and experienced socially and legally.
6 There have been several cases of adultery that involved sexual acts other than intercourse or that included same sex couplings (Cossman, 2006). These cases challenged the prior definition of adultery to be more inclusive and to focus on the perception of betrayals rather than the possibilities of pregnancy.

References

Braun-Harvey, M., & Vigorito, M. (2016). *Treating Out of Control Sexual Behavior: Rethinking Sex Addiction.* New York, NY: Springer.

Catania, J., Gibson, D., Marin, B., Coates, T., & Greenblatt, R. (1990). Response bias in assessing sexual behaviors relevant to HIV transmission. *Evaluation and Program Planning*, 13(1), p. 19.

Cossman, B. (2006). The new politics of adultery. *Columbia Journal of Gender and Law*, 15(1), p. 274.

Dunn, M., Martin, N., Bailey, J., Heath, A., Bucholz, K., Madden, P., & Statham, D. (1997). Participation bias in a sexuality survey: Psychological and behavioral characteristics of responders and nonresponders. *International Journal of Epidemiology*, 26(4), p. 844.

Farkas, G., Sine, L., & Evans, I. (1978). Personality, sexuality and demographic differences between volunteers and nonvolunteers for a laboratory study of male behavior. *Archives of Sexual Behavior*, 7, p. 513.

Marcus, B., & Schütz, A. (2005). Who are the people reluctant to participate in research? Personality correlates of four different types of nonresponse as inferred from self-and observer ratings. *Journal of Personality*, 73(4), p. 959.

Merleau-Ponty, M. (2012/1945). *Phenomenology of Perception*. New York, NY: Routledge.

Meston, C., Heiman, J., Trapnell, P., & Paulhus, D. (1998). Socially desirable responding and sexuality self-reports. *Journal of Sex Research*, 35(2), p. 148.

Plaud, J., Gaither, G., Hegsted, H., Rowan, L., & Devitt, M. (1999). Volunteer bias in human psychophysiological sexual arousal research: To whom do our research results apply? *The Journal of Sex Research*, 36(2).

Young, K. (2008). Internet sex addiction: Risk factors, stages of development and treatment. *American Behavioral Scientist*, 52(1), p. 21.

Chapter 2

Infidelity Today in the United States

> Nowadays with Ashley Madison, all the hook up apps, and other
> tools that are available, almost everyone has access to on demand sex
> with others that can be arranged discreetly. I imagine there is more
> cheating now than ever before.
>
> —Research participant

Most studies on infidelity in the US tend to use one of three types of
methodological designs and sampling strategies. These are surveys of
samples of people responding to hypothetical infidelity scenarios (often
university students); surveys among samples of people who have actually
experienced infidelity reporting on their experiences (also often university students); and analyses of cases or qualitative narratives among small
numbers of people describing infidelities that have occurred in the past.
For the first two types, the goal is usually to investigate the correlates of
infidelity, describe the differences between those who cheat and those
who do not, and to describe their impact all in terms of measurable variables. In the case of qualitative approaches, the focus is not on measurable variables but instead is on the degree to which the case or cases
might be transferable to other cases, the contextual details, and potential
meaning or interpretation of the narratives. Each of these approaches
has significant limitations related specifically to the sampling strategies
and research designs. Before reviewing the findings from the literature on
infidelity, it seems important to consider these issues to set a context for
what follows as findings from these studies.

The first type of design is problematic from a sampling perspective.
Samples of those who have not necessarily experienced infidelity evaluat-
ing how they say they would behave hypothetically is arguably not the
same as samples of people who have experienced infidelity responding
to questions about an actual experience of infidelity. This is problematic
for two reasons. It is possible that different types of people might be
more inclined to have affairs than others; therefore general population

samples are not appropriately matched to the sample to which we wish to project—those who have had affairs. We can also imagine that the issue of responding to a hypothetical scenario lacks the context and situational variables that might be important mediators of behavior and these are simply not present in hypothetical scenarios. The details of a particularly dissatisfying primary relationship, for example, and the visceral attraction to a particular other, as might be present in actual instances of infidelity, are simply not available to those who are only hypothetically entertaining the idea out of context. In addition, responses to hypothetical scenarios on all topics—but even more so for topics such as infidelity—are often shaped significantly by social desirability biases. Yet despite these limitations, samples of general populations (or a subset of the general population, such as university students) responding to hypothetical scenarios are common designs for research on infidelity. Researchers turn to these designs, it is assumed, because of the challenges in garnering sufficient response rates to surveys on infidelity among those who have had affairs, the second most frequently used design for surveys on the issue.

In the case of quantitative samples of those who have had actual affairs, there is the problem of non-response bias, discussed in chapter 1, which has been documented for many studies on sexual behavior, including studies of infidelity. We can therefore assume in this case that many more people than those who respond to such surveys, and potentially qualitatively different types of people, have had affairs than are captured in these studies. The results therefore taken from these designs may not be entirely representative of the population of those who have been unfaithful. Further, these surveys, regardless of who participates, tend to concern themselves with reductionist views of the phenomenon to the variables that can be measured (e.g. demographics, attitudinal ratings, situational variables). One can argue that these simple models are not sophisticated enough to do justice to the complex issues of commitment, human decision-making, and erotic or sexual experiences. Despite these limitations, these types of surveys have been valuable in developing a general understanding of the cluster of related variables that co-occur with infidelity.

Regardless of which type of sampling strategy is used, these quantitative designs are of limited clinical value. Knowing the correlates of infidelity for any sample group is not necessarily helpful in addressing the particular client who is experiencing a situated particular experience as he or she or they enter psychotherapy. For example, to know that factors, such as religiosity, or marrying later in life, are correlated to a decreased likelihood of infidelity (Atkins, Baucom, & Jacobson, 2001; Drigotas & Barta, 2001; Barta & Kiene, 2005) may be interesting and consistent with a particular client experience. It may also suggest underlying values and related concerns that might be relevant to explore. Yet we would certainly not suggest to a client in premarital counseling to become more religious or to marry later, or to explain to someone who has been betrayed that he or she married too early or lacks appropriate values in a therapeutic context. In the end, our clients are interested in their stories and relationships and in making meaning from their experiences in context. Clients usually want help processing their particular feelings, developing an understanding of themselves and others, and having more satisfaction in their particular relationships. These generalized demographic and psychographic statistical correlations are largely unhelpful toward these aims. Further, we must question whether or not the social desirability and non-response biases that gave rise to these findings in the first place are potentially replicating and reifying what is already expected or feared about marriage and infidelity through the research process itself.

Historically, for all these reasons, clinicians have largely based our research activities on clinical case studies, practice-based consultation summaries, narrative research, and other qualitative methods. These approaches preserve the context and details of the experiences and focus more on findings that might be useful in informing the clinical endeavor itself (Duba, Kindsvatter, & Lara, 2008). Usually in clinical case analyses, a theoretical framework is applied to the narratives collected (e.g. psychoanalytic, systems theory) as an example of how one might conceptualize the material, demonstrating assessment, treatment planning, and interventions from within that framework. These can be elegant and illustrative analyses and may be applicable and transferable to other cases; they may also be helpful to clinicians. Yet it is often difficult to know if the case or cases that have been selected are exceptional or typical, and therefore to what degree the understandings can be transferred to other cases. Similarly, a relative lack of criticality in approaching the selection of the theoretical approach to the analysis of cases is usually present. Most clinicians are not adequately cross-trained in a variety of approaches and cannot always develop research through the lens of an opposing viewpoint or clinical framework. In addition, many published clinical case studies are contained in very specific journals that align themselves with particular clinical theories and are not broadly read by others. There is a relative dearth of direction for clinicians that crosscuts theoretical orientations.

One approach, phenomenological psychological research, seeks to be descriptive and to provide an analysis of a phenomenon without subscribing to a particular psychological theoretical approach and has been used to consider the phenomenon in a more abstract and structural manner (Jeanfreau, Jurich, & Mong, 2014; Zapien, 2016). The beauty of this approach is that it is not constrained by sampling issues, as the focus of study is not on representing the people who engage in infidelity, but rather on rigorous description of the structure of the phenomenon itself through consideration of possibilities, imaginative variation, and logical principles. Phenomenological researchers are therefore not burdened by the need to secure a representative sample in order to project to a population. In addition, the analytic lens for phenomenological analysis is not a particular psychological theory but rather all that could be understood to be psychological in general, making broader understanding of the phenomenon possible for clinical application. I will discuss this methodological approach in greater detail in chapter 4. In addition, it has been used in the research presented in chapter 5 and to inform the treatment directions discussed in chapter 6. Before we delve into phenomenological methods and the findings of the studies using them, I will review the literature on infidelity, with the knowledge of the methodological and sampling issues that limit their usefulness. It is with this critique of the methods used in studies of infidelity in mind that I offer a summary of the findings from the literature on the topic below.

Summary of Recent Research on Infidelity

The academic literature suggests that infidelity is common. The prevalence of extra-marital sex (EMS), a subset of infidelity that is widely studied due to public health concerns, has been estimated to occur in 20%–55% of all marriages in the US at some point in the marriage (Atkins, Baucom & Jacobson, 2001; Campbell & Wright, 2010; Hurlbert, 1992). Eaves and Robertson-Smith (2007) reported the prevalence of EMS to be even greater—between 26% and 75%. These estimates span a wide range and likely reflect the participation biases and social desirability biases that have been found in research on sexual behavior, discussed earlier (Dun et al., 1997; Fenton, Johnson, McManus, & Erens, 2001). Regardless, even the most conservative estimate of 20% suggests that a large number of people are impacted by EMS. Infidelity, which includes EMS, is estimated to be even more prevalent since infidelity does not require sex or marriage. Researchers believe that infidelity impacts relationship structures other than marriage (e.g. domestic partnerships, couples who do not cohabitate) at equal if not greater rates, although the majority of the literature focuses on marriage and extra-marital sex, in particular.

Infidelity comes in many forms, predominantly sexual affairs, emotional affairs, and affairs that are both sexual and emotional. Within each of these categories there are long-term affairs and those that occur as singular events or acts. Infidelities also can occur in various ways mediated by technology. Some affairs exist entirely online, via chat, Skype, text, or some other form of technological interface, and the people involved never actually meet face to face (Hertlein & Piercy, 2012). This is contrasted with embodied in-person sexual or intimate activities. And there are those affairs that include some combination of both technologically assisted communication and in-person meetings, which is the most common type. Each of these categories is not mutually exclusive or stable over time. Often one type of affair may develop into another type; an affair can start out as a relationship over text, for example, and later move into the physical realm. It can also begin with the intention of having a one-time meeting on a business trip and develop later into a series of meetings. Regardless of the type or structure of the infidelity, technology often plays an important role by providing an easy method of contacting anyone directly and discreetly as an individual rather than as a member of a household, something that is relatively new in an historical sense but ubiquitous these days. For this reason, cyber-affairs and the role of technology in the beginning and maintenance of other types of affairs is a new focus for clinical research (Young, 2008). This is particularly important given the social science studies on technology use that reveal that we are more likely to give extreme (extremely positive or extremely negative) responses in a technology-mediated communication than we are to give such extreme responses in person or via voicemail or telephone (Beard, 2002). Text, email, chat, and hook-up and dating apps are therefore more likely to encourage us to divulge more hostile, effusive, or sexual responses than we would otherwise, fueling stronger responses and reactions, presumably.

A major focus of the literature on infidelity has been on differences in infidelity behavior and attitudes by gender. These studies suggest that men who have affairs are more likely to use porn, have one-time meetings, have multiple different partners, and to have sexual intercourse as part of their affairs. Women who have affairs have been found to be more likely to have email or online affairs, emotional feelings for the other, and fewer partners than men who have affairs (Atkins, Baucom, & Jacobson, 2001; Hertlein & Piercy, 2012; Lammers, Stoker, Jordan, Pollman, & Stapel, 2011; Young, 2008). It is possible, however, that these studies might be reporting and reifying norms for gendered sexual behavior and desire learned through socialization or reported through mechanisms of social desirability effects.

Historically, there has been less social permission for women to express sexual desire or to have multiple partners. This has largely paralleled the moral arguments against adultery and the tendency for women to be portrayed as temptresses in religious texts. Women who desire sex, have multiple partners, or otherwise violate sexual norms that differ for men and women have historically experienced what is termed slut-shaming, have been likened to prostitutes, have been deemed unclean vectors of disease, declared immoral, or diagnosed as nymphomaniacs,[1] a term that once appeared in the first edition of *Diagnostic and Statistical Manual of Mental Disorders* (APA, 1952). This dynamic is readily apparent in the frequent rape case legal discourse that has included victim-blaming rhetoric. The logic in these cases is that women who dress themselves in sexually suggestive clothing and visit certain public spaces (e.g. bars, concerts, city streets) are tempting men to rape them and are "bad" girls and therefore deserve it. It is implied further that men have no control over their carnal desires, as these forces are natural, innate, and related to a biological need that is gendered in how it is experienced. Sexual desire has been accepted as part of manhood, and often within these rape dialogues there is a biological deterministic argument linking testosterone and sex drive to the propagation of the species inspired by suggestive clothing and coy behavior. While there may be some truth to a biological basis for desire (Ryan & Jetha, 2011), it is also possible that social constructivist ideas might apply here, suggesting that we are taught to feel and behave according to gendered sexual scripts including both the socially sanctioned female desire scenarios (e.g. only within marriage after sufficient foreplay) or the problematic rape scenario described earlier. While this particular argument, which is a version of nature versus nurture, is not settled in the academic discourse, and may be more complex than these two dimensions, biological deterministic ideas are conflated often with views of desire by gender. These views then tend to influence research on infidelity in the form of social desirability effects and biases in interpretation of results. In addition, for those who identify as gender queer, trans*, or any other part of the gender spectrum than male or female, their experiences are simply ignored in academic research on the topic.

According to the literature, there is an estimated increase in affairs generally for both men and women and, in particular, an estimated increase for women (in particular younger women) who are closing in on the estimated rates of men (Atkins, Baucom, & Jacobson, 2001; Lammers, Stoker, Jordan, Pollman & Stapel, 2011). This is thought to be due to increased opportunity, in part due to the availability and ubiquitous use of technology, which can be used to discreetly find and communicate with potential partners; more independence and freedom compared to past eras; an increase in available knowledge about sexual health and pleasure; and advances in gynecological care including widespread availability of ever more effective birth control (Young, 2008; Lammers, Stoker, Jordan, Pollman, & Stapel, 2011; Coontz, 2006). This increase may also stem from the fact that the definition of infidelity has shifted away from penis-vagina penetration to the perception of any type of betrayal. Research therefore counts many more experiences than what was once defined as extra-marital sex. It now includes email and online chatting, emotional affairs, and even viewing porn without one's spouse if he or she feels betrayed, among other scenarios (Douthat, 2008; Cossman, 2006).

For both men and women, the literature consistently reports marital dissatisfaction to be the strongest correlate of infidelity among those who are married. Infidelity also correlates highly with subsequent divorce even if the affair remains secret (Allen & Atkins, 2012; Kruger, Burrus, & Kressel, 2009; Atkins, Baucom, & Jacobson, 2001; Zapien, 2016). Numerous studies discuss the sequelae of affairs. These include long-term impacts on any children in the household, altering their views of trust and relationship stability as adults, and impacts on society in the form of missed days of work and mental health issues that arise associated with infidelity. Divorce, if it occurs, can bring with it additional ongoing related stressors post-divorce in the form of housing issues, child custody issues, increased financial hardships, challenges with new partners, and blended families. All of these are often stressful and can impact mental health and happiness for all involved in the long term. Staying in a difficult marriage, however, can also be problematic. Depression, anxiety, and substance use feature prominently in families of those who have unsatisfying marriages (Pittman & Wagers, 2005; Kruger, Burrus, & Kressel, 2009). And staying in an unhappy marriage can also have consequences on children's mental health, can result in missed days of work, and can affect health and happiness.

It is important to remember that it may seem intuitive that dissatisfaction causes infidelity, which in turn causes divorce. This is a typical view implied by researchers, yet the actual direction of causality cannot be determined from these studies as the findings are the result of correlations. It may be the case instead, for example, that infidelity causes dissatisfaction or that people justify their infidelities with dissatisfaction in hindsight. It is also possible that infidelity is a passive way to initiate divorce rather than divorce as the consequence of infidelity. There may be other variables that mediate all of these correlates that have not been identified or are problematic to measure. There may also be different types of infidelities with different mediators in each case.

The opportunity to have affairs, financially and structurally, is also correlated with the likelihood of having affairs, as one might expect. It is unclear, however, if people set up their lives structurally and purposefully (consciously or otherwise) in order to have affairs or if having opportunities to be intimate with others leads to the experience of an affair in some way (Lammers, Stoker, Jordan, Pollman & Stapel, 2011). This was found in studies that tracked those who travel for business, have extra discretionary income, or are extroverted and socially inclined. These types of individuals have been shown through correlation to have a greater likelihood of infidelities (Lammers, Stoker, Jordan, Pollman, & Stapel, 2011). In addition, more educated people and those who marry early in life are also more likely to have affairs (Atkins, Baucom & Jacobson, 2001). Those who are religious are less likely to have affairs or to report them in research studies (Atkins, Baucom, & Jacobson, 2001; Drigotas & Barta, 2001; Barta & Kiene, 2005). All of these types of differences, while interesting, may reflect social desirability biases in reporting in that they reflect social mores. And as noted earlier, none of these will be particularly helpful in informing clinical directions for psychotherapy.

Psychologists, psychotherapists, social workers, and related professionals are trained to view affairs as potentially representative of symptoms of an underlying psychopathological disorder and not as driven by demographic categories or contextual issues. The relevant considerations related to an increased likelihood to have affairs from this perspective taken from the DSM-V (APA, 2013) might include depression, anxiety, bipolar disorders, some of the personality disorders, ADHD, and substance abuse, among a few other possibilities (Hall & Fincham, 2009). Yet, if 20%–75% of all couples experience an affair at some point—and these particular diagnostic patterns named earlier are less prevalent in the general population even if taken together—it follows that there may be something other than individual psychopathology driving infidelity.

Sex therapists and couples counselors might also take a less pathological view by considering issues that are relevant and more broadly experienced, such as porn addiction or problematic porn use, Internet addiction or problematic Internet use, sex and love addiction,[2] desire discrepancies, attachment problems, couples' conflicts, or sexual narcissism (Young, 2008; McNulty, 2013). Again, not all psychotherapists or clinicians are trained in how to address these categories of difficulties (with the exception of attachment issues), as many of these issues are not addressed within the scope of general clinical training nor do they appear in the DSM-V currently (APA, 2013). In addition, sex therapists in particular might focus instead on the sexual issues related to the infidelity. For example, they might directly consider whether or not the couple might be better served in an open relationship structure, whether or not there are sexual skill deficits, or if there are difficulties with desire and arousal that might be beneath the infidelity. Again, very few clinicians have training to assess and address these types of issues adequately.

Infidelity also occurs against the backdrop of particular socio-historical and demographic forces, and it is possible that the high rates of infidelity are related to larger social phenomena. Not all clinicians are adept at reflecting on the social context in which our clients experience their clinical issues, and yet we live in a very dynamic and important time relative to infidelity. Some of the key shifts include more people postponing or deferring marriage altogether, as well as shifts in perceptions about sex and monogamy. According to the Population Reference Bureau's 2011 report (Jacobson & Mather, 2011, para. 3):

Data from the U.S. Census Bureau suggest that more young couples are delaying marriage or foregoing matrimony altogether, possibly as an adaptive response to the economic downturn. Between 2000 and 2011, the share of young adults ages 25 to 34 who are married dropped 9 percentage points, from 55 percent to 46 percent, according to data from the Current Population Survey. During the same period, the percentage who have never been married increased sharply, from 35 percent to 46 percent, so that the proportion of young adults who have never been married is now roughly equal to the proportion who are married. Marriage has declined for several decades, but accelerated with the onset of the recession. Since 2007, the proportion of young adults who are married has declined in every state except for Alaska, Montana, and Wyoming.

Among those who do marry, there are more examples of revisionist wedding vows excluding mention of a lifetime commitment until death, instead suggesting their commitments will last until they no longer work (Cott, 2000). Some even create open relationships, poly relationships, or other non-traditional structures from the outset, anticipating that desire for others will occur and stating a willingness to include these options in their commitments (Easton & Hardy, 2009; Cott, 2000; Kleese, 2014).

These changes are seen in many types of unions. Same-sex marriage rights were recently legally supported through Obergefell v. Hodges.[3] This changed the landscape for more LGBT Americans in terms of how they might view and relate to monogamy, fidelity, marriage, and gender roles. It remains to be seen how same-sex marriages might differ from heterosexual ones in the long run and what meanings and experiences of commitment, infidelity, and divorce will arise for these groups. Regardless of the structure of a marriage, the sex and gender identities of those who marry, or what specifically is promised explicitly, infidelity or a perceived betrayal can occur. And infidelity is occurring now against the backdrop of a changing relationship to the institution of marriage.

Ubiquitous personal and portable technology use is occurring concurrently to our collective shift in relationship to marriage as an institution. This time period includes the use of various search tools (e.g. Google, Amazon, Netflix) that provide an implicit or explicit algorithm to search to get what we want. Most major consumer brands have used segmentation models or narrative descriptions of personas (composites of people who have similar tastes and values and who have similar purchasing behavior) to derive these algorithms and to market products and services based on a series of demographic and psychographic variables that match products and services to consumers. The advertising industry and most for-profit companies now have access to large data sets of surfing and shopping behavior and can serve us content based on our recent search history or demographics, Internet use, and consumption behavior. Some of these marketing endeavors support the development of algorithms and apps that promise marital bliss, perfect dates, and sexual ecstasy. While some people do experience positive results, it is unlikely that this is due to the tool itself. Regardless of whether or not they have been positive or problematic, these tools have also shaped our thinking as a group and made us more susceptible to thinking of our relationships as reducible to a series of data points within an algorithm, which will then gratify our needs. The Internet offers an omnipresent source for our gratification that we can access at a moment's notice if we should decide that our current product or partner is insufficient in some way. The problem with this is that our partner perhaps does not belong in the same category as products with fixed attributes.

The reductionist approach to relationships is incredibly apparent in the stories of the clients who are in their twenties and thirties who have largely not known a world without apps and search engines, who enter psychotherapy in my practice and report they are having issues in their relationships or with the dating process. In many of these sessions they state that their partner "is not meeting *my needs.*" These clients usually can articulate an itemized list of these needs, complete with a justification as to why those are the most important attributes, and a theory about why partners can't or won't meet them, largely uninformed by psychological understandings or relational perspectives. Many appear to have come to believe that if a partner is not meeting their needs, there must be a series of criteria that have not been matched between the partners and that if they find another partner who matches on these points, that partner will meet their needs. The original partner in effect is being perceived as someone who inherently lacks the capacity to meet their needs because of who he or she is. He or she is perceived to have fixed qualities or attributes—much like the attributes of a car or dishwashing liquid. This is in conflict with the view that each person can be a responsive subject (including the client who isn't getting his or her needs met) with whom each person can co-create another dynamic than the one that "doesn't meet my needs." This is one of the underlying ideas of why psychotherapy is effective—that people can change and that relationships (in this case the one with the psychotherapist, but it works in all relationships to a certain extent) can change and that one person can impact another dynamically, and further that relationships are one of the vehicles for personal growth, change, and development.

Similarly, in this period of search engines, we seem to have forgotten that in many cases (I would argue actually in all cases, but I won't take issue with those who claim to have a perfect match!) we can't get all of our needs or even a specific need necessarily met through one perfect match all the time, regardless of what eHarmony.com or Squirt.com claims to offer, and may have to meet them in other ways (e.g. through friends, hobbies, masturbation, fantasy). We may even have to tolerate not having them met sometimes. And these two particular ideas—that it may not be possible to meet them all or that we might have to tolerate not having them met sometimes—flies in the face of the romantic view of a perfect other, packaged as optimized online shopping algorithms applied to relationships. All of these forces combined put pressure on couples and make it much less likely that we are willing to do the work of repair and development inside of our relationships when things become difficult, as they inevitably do in all relationships at some point. It also forecloses the possibility of clients changing themselves as creative subjects in participation in the dynamics in which they engage. If they can simply go online and find someone else to meet their needs, then why bother with the work, they reason.

Another force that has come to bear on marriage, partnership, and infidelity includes shifts in our collective experiences of sexuality. In the last fifty years we have witnessed the porn industry develop from static magazine images and erotic stories to rentable videos and films, which offered sound and movement (and required a trip to a brick-and-mortar store to acquire at one point in time). Today, we have online tools that allow anyone to create, upload, download, and view porn or interact with various sexual scenarios that are available anywhere, anytime. On the horizon we can expect more sophisticated sensory immersion porn experiences and other technologically enhanced virtual experiences. In addition to the increases in porn production and consumption that parallel the increases in Internet speed and technology portability, some people are experiencing a shift in their expectations of sex, we surmise, based on their experiences of porn. Not only are the bodies often fit and attractive in porn (and we can always search to find the particular subcategories that turn us on), but we also get to control a sexual script that includes our personal version of whatever is for that moment very hot sex or sex just the way we like it through searching. This is unlike the more real experience of sex, which can be wonderful and sometimes transcendent beyond what we might expect, but also can be awkward, mediocre, or unsatisfying, and over which we have significantly less control. As a result, more and more clients are entering psychotherapy with distorted views about how partner sex should be. There are increasing numbers of cases of erectile dysfunction in young otherwise healthy men, difficulties with arousal, and more cases of couples wanting to emulate porn scenes with ever increasing complexity and intensity, feeling despondent and forlorn afterward.

It is not my intention to problematize the porn industry; if adults are having fun and there is consent between them I don't have a strong judgment about what media people consume. But what seems to be occurring in parallel with the porn explosion is the belief that all sex should be a perfect, peak experience, designed for the outside gaze and within one's control. These beliefs help set the stage for disappointment. When coupled with the "shop and search" experiences discussed earlier, this can fuel an interest in infidelity through the "meet my needs" mentality that is co-occurring.

One creative solution to this whole dilemma is coming from swingers and poly communities, which are gaining popularity. These communities seek to ethically set up relationship structures in advance that embrace the idea that we can love or be sexual with more than one or many people concurrently, that love isn't a zero-sum situation, and that we should structure our lives to accommodate these ideas if all involved agree. While this type of arrangement doesn't work for many, it allows some people to explore their needs and desires more directly without the problems of lying and betrayal.

What we know about the prevalence of infidelity, including ideas about gender differences, character strength, and situational variables, is inconsistent with current research findings and contemporary phenomena. As marriage deferment, revisionist vows, technology use, search algorithms, porn proliferation, and poly structures gain popularity, the ways in which our views of marriage, monogamy, sexuality, and therefore infidelity have changed. And because of these changes, clinical conceptualizations of infidelity treatment needs also to shift.

Notes

1 The *Diagnostic and Statistical Manual of Mental Disorders* continues to wrestle with some version of the diagnostic category of nymphomania. Currently in its fifth edition (2013) the manual includes a diagnosis of hypersexuality and hypoactive desire disorder, which often are linked to gender biases in expectations of sexual behavior. There is an ongoing discussion of whether or not to include a sex addiction or porn addiction in the manual as well. While some clients do present in psychotherapy with concerns and distress over their sexual fantasies and behaviors and in some cases these fantasies and behaviors exact negative consequences in their lives, it is unclear if any form of too much or too little sexual interest and activity is or should be a diagnosable problem and how much or how little warrants concern. Sex therapists often encourage people to reflect on their concerns and to learn to manage any subjectively understood problematic level of desire in more effective ways—through harm reduction principles, for example. Also, often the related issue of desire discrepancies within couples is at the root of hypersexual or hyposexual desire disorder diagnoses.

2 There is no consensus as to whether or not problems with technology use or/ and out of control sexual behavior should be construed as addictions. For the time being, these categories of problematic behavior are often difficult to define and are treated using an addiction framework or a harm reduction framework or with depth-oriented approaches. Researchers are working to develop clinical models of these issues. Braun-Harvey and Vigorito (2016) are well-known authorities on the forefront of developing competent training and tools for clinicians to address problematic porn use in particular. We anticipate some addition to the next iteration of the DSM to address client problems with technology, porn, and sex directly.

3 In 2015, the Supreme Court of the US, in Obergefell v. Hodges, guaranteed the right to marry to same-sex couples resting their case on the Due Process and Equal Protection clauses of the Fourteenth Amendment. A great number of same-sex couples since then have opted to marry and uphold monogamy, an open structure, or revisionist vows that modify the typical agreement. Others have specifically opposed the institution, arguing that it is assimilationist to marry. These folks take issue with the oppressive power dynamics inherent within marriage and monogamy and the hegemonic heteronormative views embedded within it.

References

Allen, E., & Atkins, D. (2012). The association of divorce and extramarital sex in a representative US sample. *Journal of Family Issues*, 33(11), p. 1477.

American Psychiatric Association. (1952). *Diagnostic and Statistical Manual— 1st edition*. Washington, DC: APA.

American Psychiatric Association. (2013). *Diagnostic and Statistical Manual— 5th edition*. Washington, DC: APA.

Atkins, D., Baucom, D., & Jacobson, N. (2001). Understanding infidelity: Correlates in a national random sample. *Journal of Family Psychology*, 15(4), p. 735.

Barta, W., & Kiene, S. (2005). Motivations for infidelity in heterosexual dating couples: The roles of gender, personality differences and socio-sexual orientation. *Journal of Social and Personal Relationships*, 22(3), p. 339.

Beard, K. W. (2002). Internet addiction: Current status and implications for employees. *Journal of Employment Counseling*, 39, pp. 2–11.

Braun-Harvey, M., & Vigorito, M. (2016). *Treating Out of Control Sexual Behavior: Rethinking Sex Addiction*. New York, NY: Springer.

Campbell, B., & Wright, D. (2010). Marriage today: Exploring the incongruence between American's beliefs and practices. *Journal of Comparative Family Studies*, 41(3), p. 329.

Coontz, S. (2006). *Marriage, A History: How Love Conquered Marriage*. New York, NY: Penguin Group.

Cossman, B. (2006). The new politics of adultery. *Columbia Journal of Gender and Law*, 15(1), p. 274.

Cott, N. (2000). *Public Vows: A History of Marriage and the Nation*. Cambridge, MA: Harvard University Press.

DeStefano, J., & Oala, M. (2008). Extramarital affairs: Basic considerations and essential tasks in clinical work. *The Family Journal*, 16(1), p. 13.

Douthat, R. (2008). Is pornography adultery? *Atlantic Monthly*, 302(3), p. 80.

Drigotas, S., & Barta, W. (2001). The cheating heart: Scientific explorations of infidelity. *Current Directions in Psychological Science*, 10(5), p. 177.

Duba, J., Kindsvatter, A., & Lara, T. (2008). Treating infidelity: Considering narratives of attachment. *Family Journal*, 16(4), p. 293.

Dunn, M., Martin, N., Bailey, J., Heath, A., Bucholz, K., Madden, P., & Statham, D. (1997). Participation bias in a sexuality survey: Psychological and behavioral characteristics of responders and nonresponders. *International Journal of Epidemiology*, 26(4), p. 844.

Easton, D., & Hardy, J. (2009). *The Ethical Slut: A Practical Guide to Polyamory, Open Relationships and Other Adventures.* Berkeley, CA: Celestial Arts.

Eaves, S., & Robertson-Smith, M. (2007). The relationship between self-worth and marital infidelity: A pilot study. *The Family Journal*, 15(4), p. 382.

Fenton, K., Johnson, A., McManus, S., & Erens, B. (2001). Measuring sexual behavior: Methodological challenges in survey research. *Sexually Transmitted Infections*, 77(2), pp. 84–92.

Hall, J., & Fincham, F. (2009). Psychological distress: Precursor or consequence of dating infidelity? *Personality and Social Psychology Bulletin*, 35(2), p. 143.

Hertlein, K., & Piercy, F. (2012). Essential elements of Internet infidelity treatment. *Journal of Marriage and Family Therapy*, 38(S1), p. 257.

Hurlbert, D. (1992). Factors influencing a woman's decision to end an extramarital sexual relationship. *Journal of Sex and Marital Therapy*, 18(2), p. 104.

Jeanfreau, M., Jurich, A., & Mong, M. (2014). Risk factors associated with women's marital infidelity. *Contemporary Family Therapy*, 36(1), p. 327.

Kleese, C. (2014). Polyamory: Intimate practice, identity or sexual orientation. *Sexualities*, 17(1/2), p. 81.

Kruger, J., Burrus, J., & Kressel, L. (2009). Between a rock and a hard place: Dammed if you do, dammed if you don't. *Journal of Experimental Social Psychology*, 45(6), p. 1286.

Lammers, J., Stoker, J., Jordan, J., Pollman, M., & Stapel, D. (2011). Power increases infidelity among men and women. *Psychological Science*, 22(9), p. 1191.

McNulty, J. (2013). The implication of sexual narcissism for sexual and marital satisfaction. *Archives of Sexual Behavior*, 42(6), p. 1021.

Nelson, T., Piercy, F., & Sprenkle, D. (2005). Internet infidelity: A multi-phase Delphi study. *Journal of Couple and Relationship Therapy*, 4(2/3), p. 173.

Ryan, C., & Jetha, C. (2011). *Sex at Dawn: How We Mate, Why We Stray, and What It Means for Modern Relationships.* New York, NY: Harper Collins.

Young, K. (2008). Internet sex addiction: Risk factors, stages of development and treatment. *American Behavioral Scientist*, 52(1), p. 21.

Zapien, N. (2016). The beginning of an extra-marital affair: A phenomenological study and clinical implications. *Journal of Phenomenological Psychology*, 47(2), p. 134.

Chapter 3

Psychotherapy for Infidelity

> You want to know how to navigate yourself out of this pain. I've got the toolkit right here. Chump Lady is not a site optimistic about reconciliation. I liken reconciliation to a unicorn, a mythical creature I want to believe in, but which is seldom seen.
>
> —Tracy Schorn, Internet blogger and self-help author

There is plenty of self-help, pop psychology, and folk wisdom available about infidelity, not all of which is supported by psychological understandings or the academic literature. Infidelity is evocative of a great number of feelings and judgments, and in many cases people touched by infidelity often find themselves in need of support. Psychotherapists and counselors of various types (e.g. licensed clinical social workers, marriage and family therapists, licensed professional clinical counselors, licensed clinical psychologists, psychoanalysts, and sex therapists) are sometimes called upon in these cases and usually will rely on clinical theory to plan treatment.

Infidelity is not a diagnostic category with a particular symptom pattern and furthermore it is not always to be the focus of treatment. Sometimes infidelity itself and the resulting feelings and issues are the presenting problem. These clients enter treatment stating that an infidelity has occurred or is occurring and they wish to address the issue in therapy. In other cases, psychotherapists are engaged to treat a different concern (e.g. relational and communication issues, sexual issues, grief, substance use) and there has also been an affair but this remains unknown to the therapist at the outset. Even if infidelity is revealed, often the clinician does not have access to the full story (nor do all the parties involved) at the outset of therapy, as the secrecy and justifications that made infidelity possible for the person who had the affair are often still somewhat present—even if the person who did the betraying is contrite and regretful. In these cases, infidelity can become the focus of treatment or may be a side issue or a symptom of other aspects of treatment (e.g. narcissism, childhood trauma, an enactment).

When an infidelity is revealed or discovered, treatment planning is also not as clear as the treatment for Narcissistic Personality Disorder or Tic Disorder, for example, might be. This is largely because infidelity is an experience that is widely varied in how it is lived. It is not a diagnostic category with a well-understood etiology or concrete behavioral evidence that would appear in session (although sometimes triangulation and secrets feature prominently in the therapeutic relationship and we can use these instances as clues to potential infidelities) and we rely on self-report largely for evidence. Infidelity can thus be treated in individual psychotherapy, couples therapy, or some combination depending on which underlying issues are thought to be related to the infidelity and the theoretical orientation the clinician uses to inform his or her practice. This book will not present a univocal approach to infidelity treatment because it is not an experience that is lived or experienced in a univocal manner. It is a complicated issue that arises and can be related to either couples dynamics and sexual issues and/or other individually experienced phenomena. Yet most cases of infidelity do share some features. Understanding these and applying them to clinical work can be helpful as a set of orienting principles. The phenomenological research presented in chapter 5 will provide these orienting perspectives.

Current Treatment Planning Considerations

When individuals present with infidelity concerns, one of the most important decisions is whether or not the unit of treatment should be the individual or the couple or both. Clinicians often make these decisions based on the theories that the clinician is familiar with, some of which lend themselves to conceptualizing treatment as a couples issue, and also the ideas and values that he or she holds personally about monogamy, relationships, and sexuality. Sometimes clients also explicitly request couples therapy or individual therapy to address infidelity, often informing the initial approach through their requests if the therapist complies with the requests. These decisions, however, might also be arguably made based on detailed assessments and in considering the therapeutic alliance.

The potential for disagreements between the therapist and client(s) on the goals of treatment (explicitly discussed or not) or between members of a couple and the therapist may prevent the formation of a productive working treatment alliance. Even if all agree at the outset on the goals and the unit of treatment of infidelity cases, these may change during the treatment as more information is revealed through assessment or as layers of issues are addressed through interventions. One guiding principle in working with infidelity is that often there are secrets and additional layers of the experience that are revealed over time. These secrets are not always withheld in a sinister fashion but rather the one who has had the affair confronts various aspects of the experience over time and reveals these understandings *to the self* over time. Treatment for infidelity therefore requires flexibility and attention to the changes that occur as assessment and treatment unfolds. Regardless, the literature as a whole consistently supports the importance of the therapeutic alliance in all cases (Sterba, 1934; Bordin, 1994; Horvath & Greenberg, 2005; Horvath, 2005; Horvath & Symonds, 1991; Safran & Muran, 2000). The therapeutic alliance is comprised of three core components: The quality of the therapist-client bond; agreement on the in-session tasks of therapy; and alignment on the overall goals of treatment between therapist and client (Bordin, 1979; Bordin, 1994). Therefore an emphasis should be placed on achieving and maintaining agreement on the goals of therapy even as they may shift, which they often do.

Creating a productive working treatment alliance is a challenge in these cases because it has been found that clinicians tend to be generally biased in their approach to setting treatment goals with clients who experience infidelity (Aponte, 1985; Hertlein & Piercy, 2008). There is, for example, significant divergence in clinicians' assessment and treatment planning decisions of infidelity issues. Hertlein and Piercy (2008) found that of more than 500 therapists responding to several clinical vignettes including those featuring infidelity, there was wide disagreement on problem severity, assessment of the problem, treatment plans, prognosis, and the targeted unit of treatment (e.g. individual or couple). These differences were found to be related to client's gender, therapists' age, therapists' gender, how religious therapists report themselves to be, and the extent of experience the therapist has with infidelity treatment, as well as theoretical orientation and training of the therapist.

Nelson, Piercy, and Sprenkle (2005) conducted a study among recognized clinical experts who treat or conduct research on infidelity and similarly found very little agreement on many key clinical treatment planning issues. For example, there was little consensus on whether or not the Internet was important as a contextual variable and whether or not online infidelities might be an essentially different phenomenon than other types of infidelities. Several important additional case planning issues—such as how to handle secrets between members of a couple in infidelity cases, if a complete disclosure is necessary or not for healing, to what degree trust is facilitated by the betrayed partner monitoring the behavior of the one who betrayed, and what treatment approaches or theoretical frameworks are most relevant and helpful—garnered a wide array of responses from experts. There is essentially very little agreement on how to approach infidelity.

In addition, therapists are biased about infidelity. These biases are generally inconsistent with the charge to provide therapy to couples and individuals in a non-judgmental manner, which is not attached to any particular outcome (e.g. reconciliation, divorce), as training and ethics codes of our professions mandate (Aponte, 1985; Hertlein & Piercy, 2008). These biases have been found to be related to therapists' personal histories with affairs, marriage, and divorce, and whether or not each of these resulted in better or worse circumstances personally rather than what might be in the client's best interests or the academic literature. The self-help industry also takes a strong personal and biased approach to dishing out advice liberally about how to win the partner back or that one should leave. The majority of clinicians tend to embrace implicitly the clinical objective of reconciliation at the outset, rather than to consider the potential value of other possible structural changes (e.g. divorce or opening up the marriage) as equally relevant potential outcomes after an affair or within any given relationship. No data exists to support that any of these directions or outcomes is inherently better or worse from a mental health perspective in the long run, yet psychotherapists continue to support traditional marriage, monogamy, and romantic dyadic notions of coupling more than other potential possibilities (Aponte, 1985; Hertlein & Piercy, 2008). This is likely a conservative approach and one that is often in the best interest of the clients as they begin therapy. (After all, one can always open up or divorce later once significant attempts at reconciliation are exhausted, so perhaps there is no need to lead with these more bold structural solutions.) However, monogamy and repair may not be the most fitting options for all ultimately. The clinician's personal preferences and values should at the very least not be driving treatment goals and structural options for others. We only really know that a decision about a relationship is a good one after the fact when there is no regret and hopefully with the benefit of some awareness of whether or not our decisions are not enactments of unmetabolized early relational material.

Because of the lack of agreement on clinical case conceptualizations and treatment planning in cases of infidelity and the difficulties with creating and maintaining strong therapeutic alliances in these cases, many therapists are turning toward practice-based research. In these cases, contemporary recent cases are extrapolated to identify more transferable and effective treatment-planning guidelines and to accumulate knowledge to assist one another in these difficult situations (Dupree, White, Olsen, & Lafleur, 2007). These practice-based studies approach infidelity from the perspective of particular psychotherapeutic orientations, usually with the implied treatment goal of repairing the relationship and returning to monogamy (Hertlein, Piercy, & Wetchler, 2005). While inspiring and often helpful, the lack of transferability to other cases—including those where clients do not wish to reconcile and repair the relationship and for use within diverse psychotherapeutic theoretical frameworks—is a limitation (Fife, Weeks, & Stellberg-Filbert, 2013). In addition, most of the published clinical treatment directions are a decade old.

There are three important and accessible texts written for clinicians somewhat recently that inform subsequent treatment directions applied to infidelity, which deserve mention here. Shirley Glass (2003), a psychologist and researcher put forth extensive research focusing on *prevention of infidelity* and the *aftermath of affairs*, a subset of what this text will address. Her very thorough text on how to recover after an affair includes sections dedicated to the perspectives for all parties—the betrayer, the betrayed, and the third person involved. Within this text, and because her audience is most likely to be the one who was betrayed, she focuses on processing feelings, protecting the marriage from outsiders, boundaries, and reestablishing trust through apology and forgiveness (Case, 2005). While all of these steps are likely to feel helpful and soothing to the one who was betrayed, there are two major shortcomings. First, they fail to take into account the underlying issues that may have driven the affair in the first place and in particular they do not address the needs of the one who had the affair who ostensibly still has some concerns or feelings that preceded the couples counseling. Secondly, they support rigid and potentially problematic aspects of marriage and sexuality.

Within Glass's model are discussions that suggest that flirting, having friendships with others who are attractive, or talking to others outside of the marriage relationship about intimate details is a threat to a monogamous relationship and must be an additional target for behavioral intervention (Glass, 2003). The implication is that marriage and partnership should be protected, that one's partner should be one's best friend with whom one shares the most intimate details only, and that all others should receive only a few details and a curtailed sense of intimacy. This is problematic in that friends and peer groups often are a very strong support for each of us individually. One relationship—a marriage for example— is unlikely to provide all one needs socially and emotionally. Glass recommends that, in cases of difficulties within couples, they should only divulge their concerns to a qualified marriage therapist or specialist. This presupposes financial and structural support for such discussions that not all couples and individuals have. Further, this entire direction of protecting marriages from outside threats excludes other structures such as open structures, polyamorous arrangements, and strong friendships outside of marriage. It also is problematic for those who identify as pansexual or bisexual. Are they to never deepen their friendships with any one at all because they are more broadly attracted to all genders and these relationships may be problematic for their primary relationship? Further, if we consider intimate partner violence and emotionally abusive marriages, it is not ideal for these relationships to be insular and closed off from other relationships as this may support further ongoing abuse and secrecy. In the end, the witch hunt of the temptress or the bad boy with whom the affair occurs and the unquestioned support for monogamy and romantic love combined with deep friendship as the pinnacle of adult social and sexual health is very restrictive, idealized, and problematic to achieve for many people.

The Handbook of Clinical Treatment of Infidelity (Piercy, Hertlein, & Wetchler, 2005) also deserves discussion here. This text offers an edited set of chapters written by various authors of varied theoretical contributions to treatment for infidelity, each of which presents a somewhat divergent approach. The chapters within discuss Emotionally-Focused Therapy (EFT) approaches (Johnson, 2005), the split self (Brown, 2005), delayed trauma (Lusterman, 2005b), accusatory suffering (Stalfa & Hastings, 2005), Kleinian object relations (Whitty & Carr, 2005), and systems approaches (Bettinger, 2005). The Handbook does an excellent job of presenting varied views and as such provides a sense that clinicians may not be able to apply one particular view to the issue. Further, EFT models, the split self, delayed trauma, object relations, and systems views are not inconsistent with the research findings presented in this text. However, each of these approaches has some limitations, discussed next.

Some of the theoretical ideas presented in this text are more helpful or more applicable to a broad range of clients and are worthy of note. One very prominent and often successful approach is Sue Johnson's EFT, which is based on attachment theory as applied to adults as a means for understanding both the trauma of infidelity and the process for its repair. EFT is a couples therapy approach primarily and in many cases is an excellent framework for those who wish to reconcile and/or work in couples counseling. It has been successfully applied to infidelity and has a theoretical view of sexuality as attachment. The main concern with EFT, however, is sometimes EFT practitioners do not have sufficient training to address the sexual side of the couples' dynamics or it may also be possible that not all sexual issues are in fact fitting cast as attachment issues. Further, not all cases of infidelity are treated in couples sessions and not all couples wish to repair their relationships.

Esther Perel, author of *Mating in Captivity* (2007) deserves mention here. Perel's work is contemporary and builds on clinical case examples and offers a perspective that is more open-minded and less moralizing than others. Her views are largely divergent from those of Johnson (2005) and Glass (2003), in that she suggests that eroticism is a key concern and not necessarily attachment and trust. She also offers a fair critique of the problematic romantic notions of marriage in the US that predictably make matters challenging for modern marriage. Her text is intriguing, broadly read by consumers and practitioners alike, and is suggestive of some directions for clinical treatment, although the guidelines are not detailed enough to direct treatment planning and they do not account for those cases where her ideas are not fitting (e.g. those that are examples of psychopathology or cases of problematic attachment).

Other notable contributions come from psychoanalysis, psychodynamic perspectives, and object-relations theories and practices, which have a long history and much success for delving into the deeper underlying issues including relational and sexual ones. These practitioners address the subconscious material, the issues of sexual fantasy and sexual desire, and the underlying complex parts of the self in a dynamic manner. These approaches have drawbacks, however. They are less accessible to clients because of their cost and the necessary time commitment. These approaches also do not typically address couples, nor do they tend to provide immediate relief from crises—often a desire when an affair is discovered.

There are many other approaches, both discussed in these texts and as understood from within a particular theoretical framework, and I will not discuss the merits and drawbacks of each here except to say that in the end, the therapist is faced with many choices in treatment planning and at the same time is not likely to be cross-trained in various approaches, to sufficiently be able to consider which of these is most fitting for the client or to combine approaches easily. Each of these authors mentioned earlier includes chapters dedicated to addressing issues of technology and the role of behavioral changes needed for the future, although these are somewhat outdated and could be refreshed for the times. They do not generally include any emphasis on divorce, opening up relationships, or sexuality concerns.

Treatment Planning in Practice

What follows are several clinical examples taken from my practice to illustrate the complexity and nuances of goal setting and treatment planning and the potential need for more flexible client-centered models that can be applied to couples and individuals more broadly. The cases have been slightly altered to protect the anonymity of the clients and represent composite narratives. What will be readily apparent to clinicians is that many of the ideas discussed earlier would be applicable to these cases and would likely benefit the clients, and yet there are a host of additional considerations that may make them unfitting.

In the following case, the role of technology in infidelity and the consideration for assessment of interest in opening up the relationship as another way to resolve the ethical dilemmas of infidelity and monogamy are considerations, and yet these ideas do not feature prominently in the published approaches to treatment so far.

A fifty-two-year-old successful and gregarious man, Mr. B, enters psychotherapy with a concern about his moral compass. He has a dynamic and vibrant professional and social life complete with volunteerism and a deep commitment to his religious community and values. Mr. B is the type of person one would like to have at a dinner party; he is witty and finds it easy to talk to just about anyone on a wide range of topics. He is newly engaged to marry his second wife and loves her deeply. They met online while he was married to his first wife. She is fifteen years younger than he is. She is intelligent, successful, and beautiful, and they have a strong connection sexually. Mr. B has a history of infidelity, however, of which he is ashamed. He is hoping to turn over a new leaf in this marriage and to honor his commitments in earnest. Since they have been together, however, Mr. B has had two one-night stands with two different women and sometimes meets with an ex for coffee or to participate in family events that they used to attend together. During these meetings often there is some intimate dialogue, hugging, and kissing. His fiancée is unaware of all of this. Mr. B wants help to avoid potential affairs in the future and to bring his current behavior with his ex into a place of integrity, as he knows he hides these meetings because they are over the line relative to what his fiancée would find acceptable.

There are two ways that his betrayals typically begin. Either he has contact with an attractive woman in some socially sanctioned business or social context and adds her to his Facebook, Instagram, or LinkedIn networks. Then, because he spends a great deal of time reading comments, viewing pictures, and posting his own on these sites, he finds himself engaging online with more intimate, flirty, or sexually suggestive comments, which he sees as fun and harmless. He finds these situations normal and innocuous, claiming that he should be able to be friendly with attractive women without it being problematic. He notes that he is inherently social and gregarious with men and women he doesn't find attractive as well. Mr. B finds himself not intending to have an affair with any of these women, but if the situation presents itself, he finds it irresistible in the moment and often only recognizes it as an affair after he has already crossed a line. He has little insight into why or how this occurs. The other way an affair has begun for him is when he travels for business. In these cases, if he finds himself with insufficient social stimulation, he will feel compelled to go online and look for a date for the night. This process also occurs without much awareness in that he begins by contacting people he knows who are traveling with him, and then if nobody is available he continues searching for something to do on the Internet, such as shopping or reading articles. One thing will lead to another and he will find himself on Craigslist eventually looking for a hook-up. Mr. B is deeply ashamed of this behavior. Often these hook-ups do not continue for long, but sometimes they develop into longer relationships that he continues on the side in secret for a period of time.

He isn't currently having an affair in the classic sense. But he wants to dispense with his shame about these experiences. He also wants to prevent this ethical dilemma of promising monogamy in his new marriage and then being unable to uphold it. He feels out of control. He approaches therapy with the expressed goal of wondering if he has a problem with sex addiction or Internet addiction. He sometimes sends articles and witty emails to the therapist describing a thought about treatment. Early in treatment he requested to add the therapist to his Facebook, Instagram, and LinkedIn accounts. When asked to reflect on these gestures he has very little response.

After two years in therapy he has some insight and has developed some skills for tolerating being alone. He has come to the conclusion that he enjoys women and flirting immensely and is exploring his needs for attention. He feels ambivalent about marriage. He is also processing his feelings about his early family life and past relationships with women. His fiancée is pressuring him to commit because she wants to have a baby with him. She gets anxious about his ambivalence. He continues to work on developing insight and emotion tolerance skills so that he might have more access to conscious choice in the moment.

In this case, most clinicians would have several directions they might consider for treatment. Some may believe strongly that honesty about the past is important and may be preventing intimacy with his wife and may insist on couples therapy. And yet he is not aware or insightful into his behavior and desires enough to have a thoughtful disclosure or dialogue that would be satisfying to his fiancée at this point in time. He cannot answer many questions about his motivations and emotional experiences even without her present. In addition, and perhaps more importantly, he is unwilling to include her in therapy. These two factors suggest couples therapy is contraindicated.

Seeing him individually could also be considered problematic because such an approach represents another split or triangle with the fiancée— the therapist becomes the outside "other" in the relationship supporting the split self that is not present in his primary relationship. Most clinicians, if they choose to work with him individually, would construct a treatment plan to help him to gain insight into his behaviors and develop emotion tolerance, and to investigate his ambivalence about his upcoming commitment among other goals. However, this case implies two very important possibilities that are not currently addressed in the usual approaches to infidelity. The first is that there are examples of people who fare better in open relationships or for whom variety, in particular sexual variety, is important. This idea is gaining support in the US, and it remains to be seen if the clinical understanding of what constitutes a split or a relational issue can become consistent with new views of sex and relationship structures. This particular issue is a value judgment that may be available to question and perhaps could be offered to the client to determine what is right for him. While this is not part of his current arrangement with his fiancée, and she does not seem to suggest to him that she is looking for such an arrangement, one potential resolution to the ethical dilemma in this case would be for them to open up the relationship either sexually or to other intimate relationships. If this is not a direction he wishes to explore, at the very least it would be helpful to consider what from among his flirtatious behaviors with others is acceptable to her as well and what works best for them. What if, in this client's case, understanding and acceptance of his desire to become polyamorously oriented and then to essentially "come out" to his fiancée about this, is the route to healing and integrity? This approach is not emphasized or normalized in the literature except as applied to same-sex relationships (Bettinger, 2005) and yet it could be relevant in some cases.

Another issue includes the potentially problematic role of technology in Mr. B's affairs. He spends a great deal of time online and uses technology to distract from many of his emotions. This is not particular to him at this time in the US nor is it inherently problematic per se. However, his notable lack of emotion tolerance skills, inability to be alone, and lack of insight into his behaviors online and with women is troubling. In the end he feels badly about his actions but seems out of control and unconscious as he is taking the actions.

One really important contemporary dialogue in mental health is whether or not technology addiction exists and how technology for some can be problematic and sometimes also related to problematic sexual behavior (Braun-Harvey & Vigorito, 2016). At this time, the clinical literature has not come to consensus on how technology and sexuality are related and what exactly constitutes a problem in this area and the treatment thereof. In this case, technology seems to lead to a quick feedback loop of validation and inspires more searching behavior, and prevents him from learning to experience and tolerate difficult emotions such as boredom, loneliness, emptiness, and fears, which we surmise are beneath the acts. Because Mr. B lacks insight into the antecedents and consequences of his behavior, and has not developed skills to encounter and tolerate a host of difficult emotions, a full apology to his fiancée or modification of the behavior would be problematic at this juncture since he is unable to explain his behavior and feelings and thoughts in session without his fiancée present. When he imagines what he could say to her, it is a charming well-crafted statement without much insight. The goal then becomes helping him first to integrate his actions and feelings.

The next case, taken from clinical practice, illustrates a couple that is very open about discussing an affair that is ending. There appears to be little secrecy about the related sexual issues that are evoked by the affair. They understand that there are many ways to resolve this dilemma. They agree that the affair is the impetus to come to therapy but that *sex* is to be the focus of treatment.

A lesbian couple is recently married after dating for two years. While they are very loving and affectionate with one another, they have always had difficulties with sex with one another. The more butch of the two, we will call her L, experiences uncomplicated frequent sexual desire for her wife, B. L is saddened but tolerant of her wife's experiences of muted desire and difficulties with orgasm during part-ner sex. They have sex infrequently and do not use sex toys because L finds them often to be too phallocentric and feels undermined in her efforts to bring her wife pleasure. B finds desire and orgasm in the context of an intimate relationship challenging—she finds the intimacy overwhelming and sees the bid for sexual engagement as an obligation to be caring and gentle and perform well for her wife's needs through being a perfect sex partner. This implies, for her, immediate responsiveness, gentle feelings, and a passionate loving orgasm. Under this pressure she tends to find it difficult to get or stay turned on and stay focused. B has been able to engage the hetero-sexual script of arousal and passion with a man in the past if there are no strong emotional feelings: "I don't care about his emotional needs, getting him off, or if he is gratified by my performance," she says. She can stay aroused and achieve orgasm through penetration in these contexts. With her wife, and with other women in the past, she simply feels pressure to perform and feels overwhelmed. She is very clear she is women-attracted and is very attracted to and com-mitted to her wife. B simply isn't clear about the reason for her lack of desire and surmises that it may be that she desires to be penetrated but cannot imagine requesting this of L. They enter therapy hoping to discover how they might improve their sexual experiences with one another, or if there are underlying issues to resolve that might help them unlock her desire.

These ideas came to the forefront on the heels of L discovering that her wife was having an online affair with a married man. When confronted, B claimed that it was easier to flirt and be sexy with a man with whom she has no real in-person relationship or no seri-ous feelings. They were able to discuss the affair and repair the trust quickly. They naturally shifted the focus from the betrayal to the sexual issues that have always been present in their relationship. In addition, they do not believe strongly that flirting with others is inherently problematic for their relationship so this incident was simply an impetus to consider the sexual issues rather than a crisis in and of itself. They agree that there is something about their relationship that is too polite and caring about one another to truly allow either of them to risk discussing their feelings about the use of sex toys. L also notes that she sometimes feels insufficient in her ability to please B and worries that the use of sex toys will make her feel worse. L is also reluctant to embody an even more masculine (metaphorically) penetrating role because while she is rather butch she finds this problematic from a gender identity and role perspective.

During the first sessions they are polite and have difficulty sharing their conflicts openly without attending to the other's reaction. They are incredibly attuned and connected and generous but unable to speak frankly. They meet once each with the therapist alone to allow each of them to talk more freely. In these sessions their specific desires and conflicts are more clearly articulated. In the subsequent couples sessions, they are able to talk more directly to one another with support and to identify ways to experiment with sex, eroticism, and their roles. They were also able to develop more capacity for conflict and to tolerate the idea of disappointing each other sexually leading to less avoidance and more intimacy.

This particular couple illustrates the importance of sexual scripts, gender roles, and sex roles to sexual satisfaction. Sex is another aspect of treatment planning that may be relevant to consider and that is not covered in the treatment literature on infidelity (Hertlein, Piercy, & Wetchler, 2005; Glass, 2003) or the DSM-V (APA, 2013). In this case, their belief was that the affair was a stand-in for the real issue that was problematic to discuss—the use of a strap-on and how it would be satisfying sexually but problematic from a gender identity perspective. The couple didn't require full honesty and apology about the online affair because their particular relationship did not include the notion that flirting with others or fantasy is a problem or that this was a threat to their relationship. The details of that particular engagement online were not interesting to them and they were quick to understand them as symbolic and related to the larger sexual issues they experience. What was difficult for them, and something they wanted to pursue in therapy, was a conversation about their desires and gender roles without fear of upsetting the other. Meeting with them individually was very helpful. This was because they were reluctant to share their experiences directly with the other present and this was a replication of their conversational style at home, which was not helping them to talk freely about their difficulties. In this case, having a secrets policy that frames what occurs when one meets individually with clients who are seeking treatment as a couple is important so as to avoid splitting and triangulation and to help guide the discussions that occur separately. The affair in this case, was fueled by their care in protecting each other's feelings and reluctance to raise their desires and concerns directly. These desires do not go away because they are not shared and instead manifested in the online affair. Once they were able to discuss these concerns without the other present and to understand them clearly, we were able to discuss them together. This allowed them to unpack the relationship between desire and gender roles and how these were at odds with the kind of sex they envisioned. This helped them to move through their sexual issues and to allow the affair to recede. The focus on sex, gender roles, and fantasy rather than the affair is also contrary to the literature on infidelity treatments, which largely assumes that the affair is an attachment issue regardless of how the couple considers it.

This next case illustrates several issues: Desire discrepancies, which are very common; asexuality as an identity, which is a relatively new identity being asserted by some and which is controversial in the literature and clinical practice; and open relationships as a potential way to manage these differences.

A couple has been married for eight years and they love each other deeply. They have always had a fairly tepid sexual connection, however. He calls their sexual experiences "infrequent but nice sex" to indicate that she is polite, quiet, and orgasmic but it has always felt controlled and underwhelming. He finds it physically satisfying and functional but not moving, passionate, or intimate. She could take it or leave it, she claims, as she doesn't really desire partner sex but can get aroused and orgasm nevertheless.

When her father suddenly and unexpectedly dies, she begins individual therapy to address her grief. Within that piece of grief work she comes to understand that she was sexually abused by him and begins the painful work of processing this particular aspect of her past. Paralleling this therapy, her interest in sex with her husband wanes even more and she becomes adamant that she is asexual and she refuses sex more frequently than ever before. She realizes that her husband would prefer to have more sex. Because she doesn't want to restrict his happiness and satisfaction and she also doesn't want the relationship to end, she decided that it is better to give him license to seek sex outside of their otherwise traditional monogamous committed relationship. They do not discuss the details of this much and simply continue without much sexual contact for several years. Later, he meets a colleague and begins a passionate affair with her and falls in love.

The couple comes to therapy because his wife does not find it problematic that he has sex with others but finds it very hurtful that he is in love with someone else. He claims he still loves his wife and wants to remain in the relationship but also cannot imagine just having functional sex with another woman without any feelings. He thought she gave him license and feels very hurt that she is now reneging on the agreement.

Desire discrepancies are among the most common sexual complaint for couples. While desire changes throughout the life course and in response to a great number of psychological, biological, and contextual factors, there are also couples for which significant discrepancies exist on the whole, most of the time. In cases of discrepant desire where both parties experience desire with different amounts, then couples therapy is often indicated and a sex therapist is uniquely qualified to help the couple work through the relational and sexual issues. In many cases, there are ways to drive eroticism and desire and there are excellent strategies for managing unmet desires. However, in cases of absent desire, the DSM-V (APA, 2013) suggests a diagnosis of hypoactive desire disorder, which implies that there is some "normal amount" of desire and that having no desire is pathological. This is contrasted to the view that is being asserted by the Asexuality Visibility Education Network (AVEN, 2017), which states that asexuality is a sexual orientation and should therefore be supported and affirmed just like any other sexual orientation. This view would be in conflict with the idea that the wife's sexual trauma or any other experience might be driving her lack of desire in this case. A referral or discussion of medical issues that may be present may also be warranted, as desire can wane in cases of medical issues. Yet those who claim the identity asexuality usually do not wish to be questioned or case managed for hypoactive desire disorder or trauma related to their lack of desire. To refer her to a medical doctor or a sex therapist or to suggest that there is a cause of the lack of desire would likely create a problem in the therapeutic alliance. The assertion of asexuality is similar to a lack of consent to delve into the sexual issues in therapy, as it is asserted as a position to be accepted rather than to be problematized or questioned. The skillful clinician would perhaps ask about feelings the wife has about this understanding and work very slowly to uncover any additional ideas about desire and the relationships, all the while maintaining the alliance.

The meaning of her husband's falling in love or maintaining a sanctioned open sexual relationship and her feelings about this would be important to address. In cases of polyamory, the issue of compersion, or celebrating the sexual and relational satisfaction of the other outside the relationship, within some limits (e.g. don't ask don't tell, don't bring her home, don't fall in love) is often a focus, as is jealousy. In this case, exploring the layers of feelings with respect to open relationships, sexuality, and love would be warranted to help this couple to come to an agreement on how to approach these difficult negotiations that they didn't fully hash out when they allowed their relationship to open up. Systems theorists might also gently work with the possibility that there is an earlier triangle to consider in her past that relates to the current experiences.

All of these case examples illustrate contemporary dialogues that the previously published approaches do not fully address. Each could be addressed from many different theoretical perspectives. Most of the time, the path chosen by clinicians is a good one and is helpful to clients—or they would likely cease returning each week! Yet it would be wise to consider these cases in a broader modern context as well. In each case, the role of technology, sexuality, or structural solutions are largely not suggested (in part due to lack of training on these issues). Some of the emerging sexual identity categories and relationship structures that challenge our diagnostic frameworks and assumptions (e.g. polyamory, asexuality) are also often not considered except in a pathological manner. In some cases they are problematic and in others perhaps we are shifting to a new series of beliefs about relationships and identities.

In addition, there is room to approach cases from the perspective of the one who has the affairs to develop understanding and transformation without driving headlong into apology and forgiveness as the first agenda item. Clinically, with the exception of domestic violence and abuse, there is no basis to suggest that divorce or staying in a relationship and working on it is better or worse than opening up a marriage or relationship nor are there any guarantees that any particular course of action will result in a better future. The choice to work it out after an affair is a difficult one and, while it is possible that healing after an affair can occur and even deepen a connection, usually revealing an affair precipitates a crisis, psychological distress, and even trauma reactions (Snyder, Balderrama-Durbin, & Fissette, 2012). The feelings of mistrust are often profound and difficult to overcome and sometimes prohibit the effectiveness of couples therapy (De Stefano & Oala, 2008). It is however a good first conservative approach to goal setting. It is important for therapists to hold hope for healing and to leverage individual work or individual sessions to facilitate getting a clearer assessment picture.

Because treatment planning for affairs has been found to be biased, linked to moral understandings that may not be fitting for everyone or every case, and viewed through the lens of each therapist's theoretical orientation, there is a need for a more client-centered and flexible case conceptualization and treatment framework. To that end, I have undertaken a series of phenomenological studies of infidelity and marriage that I will discuss in the next two chapters. These results provide a new framework for clinical case conceptualization and case planning and intervention.

References

American Psychiatric Association. (2013). *Diagnostic and Statistical Manual— 5th edition*. Washington, DC: APA.

Aponte, H. (1985). The negotiation of values in therapy. *Family Process*, 24(3), p. 323.

Asexuality Visibility Education Network (AVEN). (2017). Retrieved from: www.asexuality.org

Bettinger, M. (2005). A family systems approach to working with sexually open gay male couples. *Journal of Couple and Relationship Therapy*, 4(2/3), p. 149.

Bordin, E. (1994). Theory and research on the therapeutic working alliance: New directions. In A. O. Horvath & L. S. Greenberg (Eds.), *The working alliance: Theory, research and practice* (pp. 13–37). New York: Wiley.

Braun-Harvey, M., & Vigorito, M. (2016). *Treating Out of Control Sexual Behavior: Rethinking Sex Addiction*. New York, NY: Springer.

Brown, E. (2005). Split-self affairs and their treatment. *Journal of Couple and Relationship Therapy*, 4(2/3), p. 55.

Case, B. (2005). Healing the wounds of infidelity through the healing power of apology and forgiveness. *Journal of Couple and Relationship Therapy*, 4(2/3), p. 41.

DeStefano, J., & Oala, M. (2008). Extramarital affairs: Basic considerations and essential tasks in clinical work. *The Family Journal*, 16(1), p. 13.

Dupree, J., White, M., Charlotte, O., & Lafleur, C. (2007). Infidelity treatment patterns: A practice-based evidence approach. *The American Journal of Family Therapy*, 35(4), p. 327.

Fife, S., Weeks, G., & Stellberg-Filbert, J. (2013). Facilitating forgiveness in the treatment of infidelity: An interpersonal model. *Journal of Family*, 35(4), p. 343.

Glass, S. (2003). *Not "Just Friends": Rebuilding Trust and Recovering Your Sanity After Infidelity*. New York, NY: Simon & Schuster.

Hertlein, K., & Piercy, F. (2008). Therapists' assessment and treatment of Internet infidelity cases. *Journal of Marriage and Family Therapy*, 34(4), p. 481.

Hertlein, K., & Piercy, F. (2012). Essential elements of Internet infidelity treatment. *Journal of Marriage and Family Therapy*, 38(S1), p. 257.

Hertlein, K., Piercy, F., & Wetchler, J. (2005). *Handbook of the Clinical Treatment of Infidelity*. New York, NY: Haworth Press.

Horvath, A. (2005). The therapeutic relationship: Research and theory. *Psychotherapy Research*, 15(1–2).

Horvath, A., & Greenberg, L. (2005). *The Working Alliance: Theory, Research and Practice*. San Francisco, CA: Wiley Publishers.

Horvath, A., & Symonds, D. (1991). Relation between working alliance and outcome in psychotherapy: A meta-analysis. *Journal of Counseling Psychology*, 38(2), pp. 139–149.

Johnson, S. (2005). *The Practice of Emotionally Focused Couple Therapy: Creating Connection*. New York, NY: Brunner-Routledge.

Lusterman, D. (2005a). Helping children and adults cope with parental infidelity. *Journal of Clinical Psychology*, 61(11), p. 1439.

Lusterman, D. (2005b). Marital infidelity: The effects of delayed traumatic reaction. *Journal of Couple and Relationship Therapy*, 4(2/3), p. 71.

Nelson, T., Piercy, F., & Sprenkle, D. (2005). Internet infidelity: A multi-phase Delphi study. *Journal of Couple and Relationship Therapy*, 4(2/3), p. 173.

Perel, E. (2007). *Mating in Captivity: Unlocking Erotic Intelligence*. New York, NY: Harper Collins.

Safran, J., & Muran, C. (2000). *Negotiating the Therapeutic Alliance: A Relational Treatment Guide*. New York, NY: Guilford Press.

Schorn, T. (2017). *Blogpost: Chump Lady*. Retrieved from: www.chumplady.com

Snyder, D., Balderrama-Durbin, C., & Fissette, C. (2012). Treating infidelity and comorbid depression: A case study involving military deployment. *Couple and Family Psychology: Research and Practice*, 1(3), p. 213.

Stalfa, F., & Hastings, C. (2005). "Accusatory Suffering" in the offended spouse. *Journal of Couple and Relationship Therapy*, 4(2/3), p. 83.

Sterba, R. (1934). The fate of the ego in analytic therapy. *International Journal of Psycho-Analysis*, 42(3), p. 117.

Whitty, M., & Carr, A. (2005). Taking the good with the bad: Applying Klein's work to further our understandings of cyber-cheating. *Journal of Couple and Relationship Therapy*, 4(2/3), p. 103.

Chapter 4

Phenomenology and Phenomenological Research Methods

The method of phenomenology is to go back to things themselves.
—Husserl, 1900/2001, p. 168

Phenomenological research methods have been used to produce the analysis that I will present in chapter 5 and as the basis for the clinical directions put forth in chapter 6. Before delving into the method, it is important to provide the reader with some background on phenomenology. This background will make clear why this method has been selected and how the analysis leads naturally to a unique contribution to clinical treatment directions that can be used more broadly with many theoretical orientations applied to cases of infidelity.

Phenomenology is one of the movements in continental philosophy that arose in the early 1900s. While there are several different phenomenological research methods, Husserl is considered the most influential figure in the development of phenomenological philosophy, upon which the phenomenological research methods are based. In his articulation of phenomenology, he elaborated a description of perception, asserting that people can only really be certain about how things appear, or present themselves to, their own consciousness (Eagleton, 1983; Fouche, 1993). His point was simple but also had far-reaching consequences for our understanding and development of post-modernism and scientific methods in that he suggests that the external world (and therefore all that is studied scientifically) can be reduced to the contents of consciousness. "Realities are therefore treated as pure 'phenomena' and the only absolute data from where to begin" (Groenewald, 2004, p. 4). Phenomenology stands in contrast to the idea that there is an idealized Truth or Reality that can be studied as separate and distinct from consciousness in some objective manner, which is currently often assumed in most psychology research, particularly research using quantitative methods. While phenomenological methods do strive toward articulating a universal Truth, phenomenologists also temper this striving with a dual interest in the impact of processes of perception within the methods themselves on the findings.

Embedded within phenomenological ideas is the importance of the *structure* of phenomena or the articulation of the essences of experiences within consciousness. For Husserl (1900/2001), an important aspect of all consciousness is operant intentionality, or the process through which consciousness directs itself toward an object (or another subject) in the outside world and makes meaning. There is much nuance to Husserl's discussion of intentionality that is not important to dissect here other than to note that he discusses both active and passive forms of synthesis of consciousness (Husserl, 1900/2001). The passive form of synthesis is always occurring in a pre-egoic manner and therefore we may not be aware of or able to articulate meanings we are making in an actively synthesized manner. Clinicians will likely find the notion of active and passive forms of consciousness similar to the psychoanalytic and psychodynamic perspectives of conscious and subconscious processes, which interestingly arose at the same time in Europe as part of the continental philosophy movement. Husserl and Freud, in fact, were both contemporaries of Brentano, one of the first to articulate a version of the unconscious and whose ideas influenced both Husserl and Freud significantly (Groenewald, 2004). For Husserl, the phenomenologist seeks to be purely descriptive of the various layers of consciousness directed at an object, however, rather than to take this process further into interpretive processes as psychoanalytic thinking does.

Recall that for the purposes of the research endeavors that inform this book, I had an explicit wish to *describe* the experience of infidelity as separate and distinct from the processes of valuing or judging it or relating it to any particular psychological theory. The intention is that once the descriptive analysis is complete, it is possible to consider whether or not to judge the contents of a description or resulting structure, or to value it in a particular way or many particular ways through an interpretative process after the fact—viewing the findings through various theoretical orientations, for example. But if we are not first descriptive, we end up conflating describing with valuing or judging or interpreting in one step. Because our clients have different values and moral understandings of the issues involved with infidelity, and clinicians differ in our theoretical orientations, a descriptive analysis is very appealing to use in service of client-centered meaning making and cross-theoretical understandings of infidelity.

I used the descriptive phenomenological research method for psychology (Giorgi, 2009) for the three studies that inform the contents of this book, drawing heavily on Husserlian notions of phenomenology discussed above. Giorgi's (2009) method was chosen from among several possible phenomenological research methods, specifically for a few reasons: It offers a clearly articulated means to engage participants' experiences as a source of a more essential structure of a phenomenon. In addition, it utilizes a general *psychological* lens for analysis, appropriate to inform psychotherapeutic interests in general because it doesn't subscribe to any particular psychological theory or approach and it is largely strict with its focus on description as compared to interpretive or hermeneutic activities. This is not to be confused with the methods of clinical case studies of infidelity that tend to analyze a *particular case or series of cases*, often associated with a particular psychological theory or a particular clinician. Instead, the phenomenologist is concerned with the level of abstraction to be used more broadly within the field rather than from within particular theoretical orientations or as applied to particular individual cases. This structural analysis is intended to provide the basis of treatment guidelines for infidelity.

To this aim, I conducted three different studies. The first was conducted in 2013 and asked those who were in monogamous marriages for at least five years to discuss their experiences of deciding to marry and to uphold monogamy in whatever ways this was understood by them. This study was conducted in order to consider the importance of the original promise of monogamy and commitment. The idea was that in order to consider infidelity perhaps it would be important to consider fidelity as well.

The second study, conducted in 2013 and 2014, included an analysis of descriptions (gathered in person via audio recording) of those who had been married for five years, promised monogamy, and had an affair, conducted as a pilot project to pretest the interview process and prompt and consider issues associated with sampling and screening. The focus of this study was on describing the beginning of the affair so as to uncover the moments of transition from monogamy to infidelity. The result of this particular study informed small changes to the interview prompt and recruiting strategy for a subsequent study. In addition, because there were a number of people who came forward during recruiting for this study who did not qualify as married for five years but who wanted to discuss their experiences of infidelity, I added a third study in 2014 and 2015 with a larger and more diverse sample.

In the third study, I did not require marriage but did require some form of long-term commitment, although it also included married persons. In this sample there were participants who had other relationship structures and types (e.g. open relationships, domestic partnerships, same-sex couples) and experienced whatever they considered to be an instance of infidelity.

In each of the studies, I recruited participants through solicitations posted on three professionally oriented, highly trafficked social networking websites. My goal was a purposive sample, considered by Welman and Kruger (1999) to be the most appropriate kind of non-probability sampling for this type of project. I directed potential participants to contact me via email to review the consent form and participation process. This process resulted in a small sample in each case.

In the first study, three people responded. In the next there were also three. And in the final study there were thirty-six. A small sample, such as these, is not viewed by phenomenological researchers as problematic or insufficient, as the aims of phenomenological research is not to *represent* the universe of possible participants or experiences through sampling, nor is it to achieve *saturation* (the point at which each subsequent interview does not offer any new insight or material) through sampling, a common goal of qualitative research (Seidman, 1998). Instead, the essential structure is gleaned through rigorous methodical analysis of the generalized particular details within the narratives collected, which are then viewed through the process of phenomenological abstraction and imaginative variation (Englander, 2012). Imaginative variation is the means through which the researcher moves from what is presented to consciousness to the next level of abstraction to the structure of the phenomenon. Small samples are also often used in phenomenological methods because the transcripts gathered from these types of interviews are often lengthy and rich with detail, making for very large data sets in terms of details. Phenomenological researchers are urged to gather such detailed descriptions from which to begin this process and to utilize the principles of phenomenological analysis to support their case for the description of and constituents of the structure of the phenomenon.

For those who are still concerned about small sample sizes and the potential limitations of sampling for these studies, recall that quantitative samples are often problematic in that non-response bias is significant and social desirability biases are influential in the findings gathered in studies of infidelity. Gathering a representative quantitative sample of those who have had these types of experiences is simply close to impossible. Further, for use in informing clinical approaches, we need the depth and context within the narratives. Duba, Kindsvatter, and Lara (2008) suggest that clinicians should build theory from clinical cases to share with others. It is important to recall that clinical case studies, a prominent design in psychological clinical research, also often utilize a single case or a small handful of cases in their formulations in order to deliver detailed contextual findings to the professional discourse. This sample is actually large and more diverse compared to other qualitative endeavors that have attempted to address the issue in this fashion.

All participants who responded to the *Call for Participants* were provided with formal consent information and were screened to ensure they met the criteria for participation. In the first study, they were asked if they had been married for at least five years and were willing to discuss their decisions to marry and to remain monogamous in an interview via phone. In the second study they were to have been married for at least five years and to have promised monogamy, have had an affair (in whatever manner they would personally define the experience), and they did not have an open relationship or identify as polyamorous at the time of the affair.

These first two studies largely informed the design of the third study, since it became apparent both that there could be a betrayal within open relationship structures and that these infidelities were not substantively different in structure to the experiences for those who were monogamous. Further, the issue of marriage was also not required in the final study because many came forward in domestic partnerships and long-term relationships describing similar experiences to the married cases; it appeared marriage did not define a different experience. In the third case, potential participants were asked only to have begun an experience that they would define as infidelity but did not have to be married or in a monogamous relationship, nor did they have to be together for five years. The five-year criterion was originally used in the first studies to assure that participants were not newlyweds. Yet, through the feedback from potential participants who were screened out of the first studies, it became clear that the essence of infidelity did not differ much between the first or fifth year of marriage and that this criterion was perhaps artificial or arbitrary.

The forty-two narratives collected include responses from: Men and women, as well as trans*, gender queer, or gender non-conforming persons. Participants represent various ages ranging from twenty-seven to seventy-five and are predominantly heterosexually identified persons who agreed to be monogamous, although there are some LGB folks and a few in various types of open relationship structures who participated. In every case of open relationships, they met the criteria of having cheated in some way relative to whatever their commitment structures were at the time of the infidelity experience. The great majority of those who responded were married or domestic partnered at the time of the infidelity; a few were committed but not living together at the time of the affair. All narratives were collected in English.

The Institutional Review Board, the ethics committee at research institutions that concerns itself with human subjects protections in research, granted approval for the projects as outlined. All interviews were scheduled at a mutually convenient time after formal consent was obtained. For the first two studies, interviews took place via telephone and were audio recorded and transcribed in full by the researcher or were provided via email. Telephone interviews lasted approximately forty-five to sixty minutes. In the third study, responses were gathered via email. Participants were encouraged in all cases to provide a descriptive account of an experience with rich detail and to describe it as if it were happening rather than to focus on providing their analysis of the experience. The prompts offered were as follows. In the first case: "Please describe in detail your experience of deciding to marry." In the second and third study the prompt was, "Please describe an experience you have had of beginning an affair or engaging in infidelity in whatever way you understand these terms." These particular prompts were used in an attempt to encourage participants to remain in a descriptive mindset about their experiences. There was, in some cases, a need to follow up with additional prompts to encourage more detail at different points during the interview. When this was necessary, every attempt was made to avoid leading language or a judgmental tone and instead to offer additional open-ended prompts, such as, "Is there anything you'd like to add about that?" or "Please say more about. . . ."

Giorgi's (2009) descriptive phenomenological method in psychology was used in the analysis of the data, which is derived from Husserl's transcendental phenomenology (1913/1982). Such studies are undertaken from the perspective of the phenomenological psychological attitude. Through the phenomenological research method the researcher is urged to bracket personal feelings, perceptions, ideas, as well as past knowledge, or non-presented presuppositions, including psychological theories, about the given description(s), also known as the process of entering the epoché. The most obvious difference between the phenomenological psychological attitude and clinical interviewing is that in the former case, one also brackets clinical training and the clinical agenda that necessitates some judging and valuing processes in service of diagnosis, treatment planning, and clinical intervention. Phenomenological researchers bracket these aspects of consciousness so that "critical attention can be brought to bear on the present experience" without any additional valuing or judging or categorizing that normally occurs from within the natural attitude (Giorgi, 2009, p. 91). It is only, however, after consciously encountering the material that it can be considered and set aside or later reconsidered and engaged.

Before beginning research, it is customary for phenomenologists to consider, articulate, and then bracket or push aside experiences, judgments, beliefs, opinions, relevant training, and ideas about the issue in question. I offer this section to the reader in deference to the method, but also to give an entry point into critical discourse about the layers of consciousness that may come to bear on any issue we may study or treat—in this case infidelity. It is an attempt to make conscious presuppositions and to hold them lightly in brackets so that we might make space for a phenomenological engagement with the descriptions from the research itself. This is also a courtesy to the reader so that you may follow the thinking and consider the ways in which any additional judgment or valuing may have crept into the analysis despite every attempt to remain in a phenomenological attitude. It is also an invitation for the reader to consider what you may hold as experiences, beliefs, ideas, and judgments as well as relevant clinical training applied to infidelity that you bring either consciously or unconsciously to this text. What results from this bracketing process is an entering into a particular mode of consciousness called the epoché. It is from this perspective that I will attempt to engage the issue of infidelity in a purely descriptive manner from the case examples and research findings. I begin with the layers that I am aware of and that I can imagine might prevent me from remaining purely descriptive knowing that likely there are other layers that are not conscious or present to me in this moment. While not all phenomenological researchers offer such detailed accounts of the bracketing process, in this case it may be helpful as an illustration of what occurs before application of the method.

Reflection and Bracketing

I am a white, cis-gendered, middle-aged woman who was born in the US and raised in California to Canadian immigrant parents. I have been married for thirteen years to a Chicano, cis-gendered, man who is also currently middle-aged. We have many of the markers of a "typical" American family including: Two kids, two cars, a home, and a dog. We met when we were both teachers in an urban public middle school and both have advanced degrees and relatively busy professional lives. While we are not the first to be college-educated in our families, we are notably more educated than others in our respective families of origin. We enjoy some privileges socially due to these identities and social locations, but we also experience others to be racist or classist sometimes. While both of us were raised with some religious family members, neither of us is particularly religious or spiritual and both of us have objections to organized religion. Our values are largely not linked to moral arguments and often include some version of empathic or relational engagement with ethical issues and social and environmental concerns.

I am an existential-humanistically oriented licensed MFT with thirteen years of clinical experience, trained in the Bay Area of California in the early 2000s. I generally try to operate from within a client-centered framework, but I am happy to tinker with other approaches and interventions that I have been exposed to when the situation seems fitting. I loathe the idea of using the same approach each day with each client or anything similarly regimented, and seek to stay engaged and interested by challenging my mind to consider different possibilities and interpretations of the clinical materials presented to me. I have used somatic, family systems, structural, cognitive behavioral, or narrative approaches as well as psychodynamic theories and interpretations and collaborate freely with medical and complementary medicine practitioners when relevant and when clients provide a release to do so. I also recognize that I am not trained or steeped in any of these traditions or practices enough to do them justice fully as a specialist might. Most of my work recently is with adults and couples who are relatively high-functioning and somewhat affluent and privileged, since my practice is an outpatient private practice and I am not currently participating on any insurance panels. My clients have diverse concerns including anxiety, depression, relationship issues, stress, and sexuality. Because my office is located in downtown San Francisco, it tends to draw a high proportion of weary tech executives and professionals in the California Bay Area, and they are not representative of the demographics of US citizens. Perhaps I have a skewed perspective of clinical issues because of the clients I tend to see, the location of my office, and the training I have received or lack.

I do have one specialty that I recently developed after conducting the research that informs this book, which likely has informed my writing and interpretation of the descriptive analysis. I am a certified sex therapist through the American Association of Sex Educators, Counselors, and Therapists (AASECT), which means that I have been trained to address sexual issues, above and beyond the training received through MFT licensing or my doctoral work in psychology. This training includes up-to-date content knowledge (as of 2015) about sexuality and gender from a bio-psycho-social perspective and, in particular, provides clinical professional skills for addressing sexual dysfunctions and related issues. Many clients come to me now to address specific sexual concerns and dysfunctions or relationship issues that include sexual issues and infidelity. My clinical experience includes serving different types of sex therapy clients and sexuality issues including LGBT, poly, swingers, asexuals, sex workers, kinky clients, gender non-conforming/trans*, and a wide variety of clients with various identities and sexual practices. I have treated numerous cases of problems with desire, coming out, gender dysphoria, erectile dysfunction, problematic porn use, problematic sexual fantasies, sexual trauma, and problems with orgasm and ejaculation, as well as the psychological issues that tend to coexist with these issues. I do not, however, have medical training or psychoanalytic training, which would be relevant in the treatment of many sexuality issues. My training and experience as a sex therapist informs how I approach cases and how I conceptualize treatment. Had I been trained to take a different approach or at a different time and place in history, perhaps I would see different patterns in the data on infidelity and in my clinical cases. I am a product of time, place, and experience. Some of my challenges to the previously published treatment directions are largely a result of shifts in views on marriage, sexuality, and sexual identity that have come about in the last decade and through the use of technology and that I hear about in my clinical practice, in the media, and notice in my surroundings.

On a personal level, many people in my extended family have been unfaithful in their relationships and marriages, so I have learned through either their first-hand confessions or second-hand discussions. In the telling of these stories, there was always a plausible narrative complete with explanation and justification for why the infidelities happened. One family member cheated because he thought his wife was withholding in some way. Another cheated because he was cheated on by the spouse beforehand and felt this would be satisfactory revenge. Still others felt underappreciated or ignored and sought to gain attention or validation through an affair. Alcohol often seemed to be present when the affairs occurred or was to blame in these stories, or they occurred during business travel or circumstances that physically separated the spouses for some socially sanctioned reason.

These affairs impacted me negatively in several ways in that they resulted in feelings of disillusionment (or some would say, realism) about marriage and commitment and also provided shame about the nature of the character of my family members. More concretely, while it is difficult to say that affairs *cause* divorce, in many instances in my family, parents, grandparents, aunts, uncles, and other family members divorced, and the divorce, if it occurred, co-occurred with the affairs or occurred just after they were revealed or discovered. In many cases, whether the affairs were discovered or not in my family, or they resulted in divorce, the people were happier afterward, in that they eventually found what they understood to be other, more suitable mates or reentered their relationships with more skills, a renewed commitment, or more stability in their marriages. Because all of them married early or otherwise had very little experience with sex and relationships prior to marriage, it made sense that they might be happier choosing a partner later or revisiting their commitments with more information and experience to guide them. I, as a result, made my decision to marry very carefully. I was also careful to amass enough dating experience and relationship experience to inform what might work best for me beforehand. I did not marry until I was thirty-three, somewhat later than most of my peers.

I have never had an affair myself, as I would define one, and as I think my husband would define one. I am also aware of how problematic it is to define infidelity in terms of a set of concrete behaviors and, further, how little intersubjective agreement we seem to have on what constitutes infidelity, as discussed in chapter 1. In my case, I *think* I am clear about what would constitute an embodied physical sexual breach in our relationship and I have never crossed this line. Yet I am also aware of the many exchanges of words, gestures, feelings, emails, and so on that

I have had with others since I have been married. These include experiences with others with whom I sense there is an erotic, sexual, or intimate atmosphere. I don't generally discuss these experiences with my husband, although sometimes I do if they are significant. I don't keep experiences from him out of an intention to be secretive, but rather they are omitted because these engagements of flirting or friendliness with others seem to me to be innocuous and in control, within the realm of pleasant interactions that one has with others who could be potential sexual partners theoretically because they are peers and are proximal. I am careful to control my exposure to and reactions with others with whom there is this felt sense of attraction or erotic energy. In addition, these feelings are usually not felt strongly; they are fleeting sensations or ideas. I am careful because I wish to honor my commitment and because I think that these feelings can build if tended. I am not certain that I always perceive these situations accurately, of course, and the more I study infidelity, the deeper the questions of our collective ability to discern these types of distinctions seem to go. It is entirely possible that these interactions, or even others that I wouldn't categorize as erotic or intimate, might be interpreted by my husband as problematic. I remind myself that small instances of friendliness or flirting seem normal for us to engage outside of our relationship and are therefore permissible. I also know that erotic feelings or interest in others is expected to arise from time to time and is separate from my choices to engage or act on any of them more deeply. I consider my commitment to my husband more important than pursuing any given feeling or relationship in the moment. Generally, I think I am aware of feelings of eroticism and attraction I have, largely honed through sitting with clients, where we practice considering and navigating wide ranges of various feelings, including erotic ones, within transference and countertransference reactions. I may not be as skilled as I think I am, however, and it is likely that some of my feelings, reactions, and responses remain inaccessible to me consciously or are categorized by me as harmless when in fact they could develop into something problematic.

Just to be clear, these kinds of engagements are not generally overly salacious deeds, particularly sexy, in my estimation, or designed to engage with particular individuals in a secret manner with the intention to develop into infidelities. These are small gestures, fleeting thoughts, compliments, and jokes that are largely fitting for a workplace or public social scenario—with a few notable exceptions. I have had what I would characterize as crushes, yearnings, or fantasies at various points in my thirteen years of marriage. For me this is relatively rare and usually time limited (passing moments over a few days or weeks). In these cases I can usually deliberately either distance myself from this person or get to know them better, and this usually results in them becoming less of a fantasy. Alternatively, so far I have been able to analyze these feelings and interpret their meaning for myself and then sublimate the yearnings in another way. While I am always surprised by these feelings, they seem to me to be part of the human experience for many of us. I tell myself that there are many interesting people in the world and once in a while I will meet one who is truly engaging. I don't actually wish to change the structure of my marriage. I would not want to betray my husband, nor do I have the energy and time for an affair in a pragmatic sense.

My guess is that my husband also experiences these types of feelings and holds some line for himself, although we have never discussed the nature of the line in great detail. He is relatively private, playful, but also a responsible man, from my perspective, and one who was, like me, also deliberative in his decision to marry. I imagine that his innate playfulness comes out in the form of flirting and enjoyment not only with me but also likely with others, including attractive others. My hope is that both of us are aware that boundaries are needed for our particular arrangement and that despite any feelings we might have we have agreed to manage the boundaries so that they do not become problematic for our particular structure. I also imagine that he is good at changing the channel and staying focused on our relationship based on how I see him manage his attention in daily life.

Given the statistics of the prevalence of affairs in general, I do not delude myself, however, into believing that an affair is not a possibility for either of us, or anyone else, for that matter. None of the clinical examples or family stories I have heard include the idea of someone planning to cheat. They all assume they will remain monogamous or will hold to their particular agreement. This is in part why I am interested in the decision-making process or experiences people go through as they engage in the beginning of infidelity.

If I began an affair, I would be ashamed of my actions and would find myself consumed by what I imagine to be a confusing period of self-reflection. I would be devastated if my husband were to begin an affair and this would trigger much mistrust, anger, and hurt in me. In fact, I think in either case, I would feel and behave similarly to my clients; it is easy to empathize with them. Ideally, I would hope that if my husband or I were on the precipice of infidelity that one of us would find an ethical reason and the fortitude to discuss the situation before taking any action. I also hope that we would divorce if we found ourselves unhappy and had tried to work on the issues "enough" before engaging in an affair.

I am not actually personally neutral to infidelity even though I am attempting a phenomenological analysis, which requires pushing aside my judgments. My judgments are perhaps less strongly negative because I believe that infidelity is part of the human experience; however, I do judge infidelity. I don't take issue with affairs because of objections to sex, desire, or non-monogamy. I reason that desire is natural and we don't always control the object of our desires but we do control our actions on these feelings. I also think that monogamy may not work for everyone and may not inherently be a better relationship structure. I don't happen personally to be in an open structure; it's not how I am inclined. I am completely familiar with the usual and likely span of intense desire and passion and utter flat desire that we all might have at different periods over the course of a relationship or a lifetime and all the struggle that comes with this territory. It makes perfect sense to strive toward passion and desire and at other times to completely eschew sexuality even if we don't always fully understand the reasons. Many people, including myself, have some sexual desires that remain unmet in their relationships. I am sure that I am not perfectly satisfying my husband's every desire as well. In fact, I wouldn't want to, not because I am withholding, but because to fully satisfy each other's every desire reduces one or the other to an object. For me, mutual subjectivity and permission to be both subject and object at the same time is important and this naturally brings about disappointment sometimes; we will not always be perfectly attuned and aligned to the other if we are also attuned and aligned to the self.

I often frame infidelity for myself not as a sexual issue—although there are aspects that are largely sexual—but rather as an existential issue of choices being foreclosed and desire and aliveness feeling limited. This fuels affairs that attempt to transcend the steady march toward death and the aloneness we all sometimes experience. Sometimes I fantasize not only about another person sexually, but also about other careers, lives, and circumstances as a way to transcend the limitedness of it all. Within the issue of infidelity, however, is the experience of betrayal of trust, by definition. The spouse who is betrayed did not consent to be part of an open relationship, therefore the option to consider and consent to such an arrangement is withheld from him or her. His or her subjectivity is diminished and choices are foreclosed for him or her in this particular situation. One could make the argument then that I am relatively anti-affairs, seeking to prevent them or to judge them negatively because of the secrecy and betrayal of the non-consenting party in the triangle. And this is true in most cases. And yet in chapters 5 and 6 I give examples of some marriages that are stable and happy specifically because of an affair that satisfies or strengthens some aspect of the dynamic and it remains secret! The secrecy of the affair actually protects the marriage or is rationalized through what might be considered a higher-order moral argument. These types of situations give me pause and renew my commitment to client-centered therapy informed by humanistic-existential theories. I realize that while I would prefer that people make commitments and keep them, talk openly about their needs, and work toward improving things when they are not working, or exit honorably without a betrayal, I realize these decisions and commitments are not univocal or fitting for everyone. In the end, these are not my marriages or relationships and therefore my beliefs about what is "good" and "healthy" is somewhat tangential.

It is with these personal reflections that I will begin to enter the epoché and push aside my social identities, experiences, training, beliefs, and opinions and view the data from a descriptive perspective. I ask the reader to consider ways in which these personal ideas may creep in despite all good intentions. And I invite you similarly to consider all the beliefs and ideas you may have about infidelity that may cloud your views. As we enter the epoché together, our task is to consider the narratives unto themselves and to methodically describe their structural constituents without addition or subtraction of any non-given meanings.

Giorgi's Phenomenological Research Method for Psychology

By way of a more concrete description of the method of analysis, I offer the following steps to illustrate how one moves from narrative text to the resultant structure in a phenomenological study. Once the data are collected the process for analysis of all three studies occurred as follows, as described by Giorgi (2009), from within the phenomenological psychological attitude, or the epoché:

1. Read transcribed descriptions for a sense of the whole.
2. Determined meaning units. The texts of each transcript were parsed at particular points, to form a discrete meaning unit if, at this particular break, there was a shift in the psychological meaning of the content. This was done to facilitate the transformation of the data, which considers only one meaning unit at a time at this stage.
3. Transformed each participant's natural attitude expressions into phenomenologically, psychologically sensitive expressions. Each meaning unit was carefully considered as a description of a lived experience that was then restated in a more psychologically essential manner.
4. Transformed eidetically with the help of imaginative variation adapted from Husserl (Giorgi, 2009): "[A]n eidos, or a generalization that sets boundaries for possible instances of occurrences because possibilities are considered" (Giorgi, 2009, p. 197). In this step, the process included a reconsideration of the first transformation, and the empirical details of the specific experience were varied and abstracted in the effort to discover a more fundamental psychologically meaningful experience across participants.
5. Identified the structure of the experience including its constituent parts. Those items that were similar across participant descriptions

(now transformed eidetically) were considered as elements or constituents of an underlying more essential structure of the experience in question. According to Giorgi (2009), "An important criterion . . . is whether the structure would collapse if a potential constituent were removed. If it does, the constituent is essential" (p. 199).

The phenomenological analysis presented in chapter 5 provides the basis for a new view of infidelity upon which clinical approaches can be built that are more flexible and applicable to a variety of clinical cases and client perspectives and from within a variety of theoretical perspectives presented in chapter 6.

References

Duba, J., Kindsvatter, A., & Lara, T. (2008). Treating infidelity: Considering narratives of attachment. *Family Journal*, 16(4), p. 293.

Eagleton, T. (1983). *Literary Theory: An Introduction.* Oxford: Basil Blackwell.

Englander, M. (2012). The interview: Data collection in descriptive phenomenological human scientific research. *Journal of Phenomenological Psychology*, 43(1), p. 13.

Fouche, F. (1993). Phenomenological theory of human science. In Snyman, J. (Ed.), *Conceptions of Social Inquiry* (p. 87–112). Pretoria, South Africa: Human Science Research Council.

Giorgi, A. (2009). *The Descriptive Phenomenological Method in Psychology: A Modified Husserlian Approach.* Pittsburgh, PA: Duquesne University Press.

Groenewald, T. (2004). A phenomenological research design illustrated. *International Journal of Qualitative Methods*, 3(1), p. 1.

Husserl, E. (1913/1982). *Ideas Pertaining to a Pure Phenomenology and to a Phenomenological Philosophy: First Book.* Norwell, MA: Kluwer Academic Publishers.

Husserl, E. (1900/2001). *Logical Investigations.* Ed. Dermot Moran. 2nd ed. 2 vols. London, UK: Routledge.

Seidman, I. (1998). *Interviewing as Qualitative Research.* New York, NY: Teacher's College Press.

Welman, J., & Kruger, S. (1999). *Research Methodology for the Business and Administrative Sciences.* Johannesburg, South Africa: International Thompson.

Chapter 5

The Structure of
the Experience of
Beginning an Affair

It wasn't something I planned. He was a regular guy and we saw each other from time to time at the office. He was friendly and professional and sometimes funny but otherwise he did not stand out to me. One day when we were talking I recall looking over at him mid sentence and realizing that he and I shared an understanding of a situation. It wasn't a particularly intimate conversation or anything, the content was mundane and harmless. But I remember looking over at him and seeing him differently. It wasn't that he was suddenly more attractive objectively (although he also wasn't repulsive); it was the feeling that changed. He was sharing a unique perspective on a work problem that was creative and delightful to me and he was voicing an idea that I had thought but was too scared to share myself. In that moment, it was as if I had found a kindred spirit. My heart felt something strong in that moment but my mind knew this was ridiculous. He became animated for me in a different way in that moment and from then on, I could neither ignore how I felt about him and at the same time I had to make sure that I kept these feelings in check.

—Research participant

The findings discussed in this chapter have been gleaned from the studies discussed earlier. Phenomenologists are less concerned with the particular details of any given narrative and are more concerned with the abstraction of the particular to an essential structure through the process of analysis; it is important to get a flavor from the raw data that inform the findings. Reading raw texts carefully and in entirety is the first step and is offered to the reader so that you may follow along with the process. In addition, the raw texts are most like what might occur in clinical discussions in that descriptive narratives such as these—albeit usually punctuated with remarks from psychotherapists or moments of self-reflection and intervention—are commonplace in clinical practice. All of the information that follows is verbatim; however, identifying details such as names, cities, locations, and professions have been changed to protect the anonymity of the participants.

We begin with one description of an affair from a research participant, which he claims began as a friendship online and only later became sexual. In addition, there is a discussion of the role of technology in the development and maintenance of the affair and a concern of judgment and addiction threaded throughout this description that is interesting considering that technology addiction and problematic Internet and sexual behavior are contemporary issues in their early theoretical development.

> This goes back about ten or more years ago. It literally started because one of my kids got interested in doing chats online and as paranoid parents we had issues with that because we tried to get across the danger of "you don't know who you are talking to. They could portray themselves as x and they could be y." And the kid stopped doing it. But I got a little bit curious and I made a connection with someone but I have no recollection about how that started. I started chatting with someone and she was from a little town in Maine and I found it kind of nice to make a friend. I think it was a time when I needed a friend and I found it nice to make a friend.
>
> It started becoming a lot more than that and we started talking more often and I found myself talking at times when I knew it was not right because I had to make an excuse and kind of hide out. There was really no conversation about it becoming any more than that. It just literally started as she needed a friend and she was a person in a little town and didn't have much of a life outside of her work and family and we talked more and more and I started feeling very connected.

> *Researcher: Describe that connection*

> I think at the time it was a time when there were a lot of issues in my marriage and I was really lonely. I think I felt, not lonely talking to her. Even though obviously in hindsight I could have been (huh, laughs) talking to a robo-machine talking back to me. The whole weird thing about chat, is that you assume there is a person on the other end (I mean I know there was but . . .), uh, but I think that connection was, I think I found someone I could bitch to or moan to or confide in and she could do the same with me and it became I guess what you would call a friendship, but a friendship with another woman that you don't know, when you find yourself at 10:30 at night, when your wife has already gone to sleep, is not really a friend. And it's easy to say that now as we talk but then it was alluring; it was getting addictive. I can admit that to myself. I almost needed that fix to talk to her, for whatever reason. It never did become sexual on the chats, not that I remember. I don't remember it ever . . .

I don't think we did dirty talking on chat. It wasn't like we were having phone sex or chat sex. I think it was just becoming a friendship where it sucked up more and more of my time and it was no problem for me to go and chat with her when I should have been in the other room. I remember times when something was going on and I had to get on the chat and talk to her.

There was some point where she had been talking about moving down here. And a lot of it was, you know, she had always said that was something she wanted to do and she had said that her life was a zero. I think at the time she was a thirty-some-odd-year-old woman who had had no male relationships and um, I don't even know if she was sexually active. I really think she went to family and friends and worked and she had talked about moving here and there was a point when she said she was coming down and she didn't say we should get together. She didn't say anything like that. And I knew she was coming and I had a fight with my wife. And I don't know which came first, I don't know if I had a fight and then said I should go meet her or if something in my head was saying I should go meet her so I had a fight. Um, you know. . . .

So your wife knew that you were chatting with her . . .?

Her name was M by the way. Um, no I was chatting with M. She knew nothing about it. That night that everything happened I knew M. was flying in to my local airport and I either created a fight or a fight happened and I went to the airport and met her at her gate. And I went back to her hotel and still don't think she was expecting anything and then it just happened. I mean, sure, two people have to be in the same place at the same time for it to happen, but it just happened. At that point in time, I think that whole addiction, alluring, connection, I needed it. I think all those filters just got turned off. I think it wasn't right or wrong. I think at that point in time all the filters were just shut down. It's a little bit like you know you shouldn't be drinking but once you take a drink you just keep drinking. After that I know I'll have a hangover and that I shouldn't have done it or I'm an alcoholic. In a way, I, uh, really started questioning myself, because I think I am a good person and I have morals and I hold others to a high standard including myself and then here I was doing this but at that time, none of those things were in my head. At that moment, you could almost say, it was really out of body.

And the problem was it wasn't just then, just so you know, this went on for years. It wasn't a one-night stand. Yeah, for years. This is not easy to talk about. And what is difficult about the whole thing is you find yourself lurking and sneaking and lying and doing things you would never tolerate or do. And I would also say to you that anyone who says they wouldn't do it again is a liar. If you asked me if I would ever do it again, I would say hell no because of the pain it created for a lot of people. Still now, it changes everything. Um, yeah, I absolutely think it could happen again. It hasn't presented itself, but I think it's probably not all that hard nowadays to have a physical affair. Whether you pay for it or it's emotional, I don't think it's all that hard, you can go online and find a sex friend, you know, nowadays. I haven't done that but I know you can. It's just the world we live in. I don't know . . . it's like for an alcoholic. I hate to say they're the same and I've had this discussion with my wife and other people, but how does an alcoholic live with the fact that they're an alcoholic and could stop being sober five minutes from now. I draw the parallel to addiction. I have been seeing a counselor ever since this started happening. I still go to her. It's been that long. It's helpful in the sense that when things are adding up, talking to her helps me let off enough steam so that I don't act out. Can she fix me? No. I need to grow and deal with some things in my life that I've been saying to myself forever because it's easier to just not to. Is it an addiction? For me it was. I needed the fix. And then it got to the point I didn't want to hurt her feelings and it exacerbated it and that's even worse because there's no happy ending.

And my wife found out and it literally got to a point one day when I was at M's house that I either needed to come and get my stuff and move into M's house, or come home and break it off with M and whatever that meant. And I did the latter, um and in hindsight, sigh, my counselor asked me was I in love with M. And I don't think I was, I think I was in love with someone adoring me. It's a really complicated question because it doesn't mean you don't love the person. In love and love are completely different things. I'm sure you . . . I loved my wife during the whole thing but it's a hell of a way to love someone to be screwing someone else. I can talk flippantly now about it but then I didn't really see that I was hurting her. I didn't. She was at home and she was my wife and I got my emotional and probably physical needs met with this other person. Our marriage was screwed up and our marriage is still screwed up. I think everybody's marriages are screwed up.

I met my wife in the seventies. Well, I was young in my early twenties, I would have been twenty-two when we married. I think. I'll tell you a quick story. I met her at a summer camp. It was a little surreal. It was a month in the wilderness. We met and it was one of those things where I was just really attracted to her at this camp. And when I got home my mom is like, "Did you meet anybody?" and I was like, "No, just R" and then I kind of pursued R and she wasn't interested at that time so she introduced me to a friend of hers, P, and P and I fell head over heels. Someone she had worked with . . . and I fell head over heels with P and it drove R nuts. And eventually, R kind of worked her way back in. I mean P and I are Facebook friends at this point in our lives and R doesn't know, but there's nothing going on with P. P's been married for twenty-something years and has kids but um, I think R and I were probably meant to be friends. And we were forcing it for thirty years. We have two great kids and. . . .

You know, in a perfect world you would treat a marriage like a business deal. After five years if there's no use or it's not working you just let people go. But there are too many emotions. My wife is one of these people who believes that the concept of monogamous relationships is stupid. Not that she's a swinger, far from it, but I think she thinks that people weren't expected to be together for life. People change and people's needs change and people come and go. She doesn't like intimacy. She's never liked intimacy. It's just created a lot of connection issues with us. Um, and look when the kids were little things are different. Everything is focused around kids 24/7, which is why a lot of people . . . you know look, I think my wife sometimes had the attitude that. . . . Look, I'll be honest with you I need the emotional connection and while sex was good I really think I had an emotional affair that turned sexual. It wasn't just a matter of me getting off. I really believe that. I still look for that emotional connection—and get it or don't get it—but I still look for that. It would be really interesting to wire us at the time that all of these situations are mounting in intensity to see if the endorphins are different. I snuck and lurked and lied and manipulated and I got really good at it and it's something that just makes me ill thinking about because it's not a part of me that I'm terribly proud of. And whether you call it addiction, I'm not a psychologist by any stretch of imagination, what I said and did were a lot of things . . . I mean I went on a business trip and she came with me and I went and did my thing and when I came back she was at the hotel. And I was on a business trip! I mean my wife does not know all these gruesome details.

And that's fine, but you know I am having some situations at work right now. I had a paycheck that did not go through and I'm having another one issued and R is coming unglued about it because you know she's concerned, twice in my life I've had jobs disappear, and there were things happening with the company or reorganizations and she's pretty freaked right now and she actually made a comment about M this morning. Because I've been emoting to her a lot because I'm frustrated with what's been going on in the office and she said this is the kind of point in your life when you started talking to M. My wife's reaction when I'm emoting a lot, is like just go fix it and there are times in your life when you have to scream and you don't really want a solution you just need somebody to hear you. She's not terribly sympathetic. "The last time I wasn't very sympathetic you went out with M." So it still has ramifications. It's hard to talk about. I think I looked at your call for participant post for about fifteen minutes before responding. And what I struggle with now is that my marriage still sucks and my wife still brings up M because the same issues are still there. She's like "I've always been like this and if you don't like it you know where the door is." So, it's pretty stuck. And I'm not sure if I want to leave.

The phenomenologist continues to read all of the narratives and at this stage will abstain from the next steps in analyses despite the tendency to see patterns or make meaning from initial readings or narratives. We proceed then to another narrative that includes a woman who has a sexual relationship outside of her marriage, which she does not consider an affair. Yet she continues later to describe another subsequent experience that included both sex and love, and this she does characterize as an affair, although she also takes issue with labeling experiences of infidelity altogether. She clearly expresses her sexual frustration and her reasoning for the events and highlights how difficult it may be to come to intersubjective agreement on what constitutes an affair more universally.

I'm gonna try to not be metacognitive about this or like, totally overly analytical. I guess the first experience that I had, uh, with I guess what would be considered an affair would be . . . I guess I had been married a couple of years? Like maybe two years? Or so. . . . And my two upstairs neighbor boys, who were just a few years younger than me at the time, had come down, and you know, we were hanging out and partying a little bit and um, one of the guys ended up just kissing me. And you know I kind of . . . I was really taken aback by it. Right? I didn't think anything of it but I just remember thinking how hot it was! And how turned on I got! And we would have probably gone a little bit further, um his hand was like down my pants and up my shirt just a little bit and his friend interrupted us in the bedroom and we stopped. And, um, a couple of days later he ended up coming downstairs and we ended up having sex.

And I think for me . . . the like the beginning of an affair, I guess, I kind of didn't really consider it sort of like an affair? . . . until I started seeing this guy on a regular basis. And um so, I think, you know, that was my first experience with, you know stepping outside of, of my marriage with my husband and you know I'd already been really unhappy. . . . Like our sex life was nonexistent and um I . . . so for me it was like that initial . . . like when he first kissed me you know, and kind of felt me up, it was that initial like WOW, this was really exciting, but I didn't really consider it cheating, you know? I just kind of, just dude, I because I was like wow, like truly the intention was on his part and not mine and he really surprised me out of the blue by kissing me, right?

But when I had him come down those couple of days later and actually intended on having sex with him, and you know, got showered and dressed in lingerie and had condoms, to me that was when a sort of at least an affair in my mind began because the intent in my mind was to connect with someone other than my husband and by connect I mean sexually connect. This was my first taste at being very agentic in my sexuality and saying, "I wanted this!" You know? Although he hit on me initially, I wanted this. I ended up . . .

Let me back up a minute . . . my husband at the time and I . . . just a very quick background. . . . My spouse and I were students and he's from Brazil. I married him and I'd just turned twenty-one. I'd been with girls before and one guy. And so the whole heterosexual like marriage thing to me was very, um, very different but very exciting and something that I was excited to try but I didn't really have something like a template. I didn't know how to be in that relationship but I have always been such a sexual person and I kind of have a tendency to separate sex and love and so for me those first two years of marriage where things were very rough for a variety of reasons, you know, new marriage, you know, language stuff, you know, we were living in a . . . like we were just starting out, you know? And I kind of, like I knew that sex was so important and I couldn't kind of figure out what was going on but I had to know in my heart that it wasn't me. I was like, dude, because I hadn't had issues before, you know, with the few partners I had in my life. And so he and I struggled those first couple of years. I was like, "It's gonna get better." I was in grad school and I thought we just needed to kind of like iron things out and it'll get better and so when the upstairs neighbor hit on me it just kind of validated these feelings that I had that I was desirable and that I was worthy of sexual attention and I was worthy of a man's affection and desire and that's why it took me so off guard, caught me so off guard.

But that's why a couple of days afterwards when I started to think about it I was like, you know, I was just like, fuck it man, I am sick of like waiting around for this to happen and this just feels good. Like for once this just feels good. It just felt really, really good. And so that's why I said, you know . . . I didn't think about this as being a one-time thing or a multiple time thing I just thought about it being like, come down and let's make this happen. And I think that, now looking back reflecting back all those years ago, I have to admit I was excited. I was excited that somebody showed interest in me like that and he was attractive and um I think that as I continued to sort of see him I realized how much I missed sex and how much I missed intimacy and physical connection and how I wanted that in my life. And of course I wanted it from my husband and I thought in the meantime maybe I should just do my own thing and when we reconnect however we reconnect then that can kind of go by the wayside.

We were married for ten years and separated for two and I think that, you know, really early on, and now that we are divorced he told me that, he said, "I kind of checked out really early on." He came to America, things were really rough and he just kind of checked out and I didn't realize that at the time. I was trying to make this marriage work, I mean I'm a committed loyal person, you know, I'm like a Taurus, you know? I'm stubborn, like I'm gonna make this work! What we both kind of . . . at least now looking back what I now realize is that he wasn't in a place to handle who I was sexually, what I needed sexually, and emotionally and physically, and I kind of wasn't in a place to handle what he needed, especially emotionally. And I think that my sexuality was very threatening to him and I think that he was the one partner of mine who has used sex as a tool and purposefully withheld sex because he knew that was what I wanted.

And so from early on . . . I was really frustrated because I was studying psychology in graduate school and I was like you have got to be kidding me! Right? Really early on I said you know I'm just going to do my thing on the side and so I'll just have this social emotionally monogamous relationship. And I'll just have lovers. It wasn't an ideal situation but it became this sort of like way of being that I couldn't. . . . Like sex is too important to me and the times that we would reconnect were . . . um. . . . We went to some counseling for a while and then he ended up starting an affair which was really devastating because that was during the time when I really had 100% committed to him and I'd broken up with the people in my life and I was kind of monogamous with him for about a year and that's when I'd found out about a situation that he had started. And I know now looking back, this is maybe TMI, but looking back, I know now that I was much too forgiving of him during those times because I knew what I had done.

She continues to describe what she considered to be an affair. The definition is an interesting part of her description and further highlights how subjective these ideas may be and how they change over time, potentially. She also later considers opening up her relationship but does not really discuss this option in much detail with her husband, assuming that it wouldn't work and instead continuing with the infidelity. She continues:

> There was one other person that I'd become emotionally connected with and that to me was more of an affair because there was that emotional connectedness as well. Before it was just kind of sex but I kind of fell in love with this guy while I was married to my spouse and that in my mind is probably the big affair that I've had in my life. It was the guy who hit on me—the upstairs neighbor—it was his best friend. So, um, in fact we still see each other every once in a while, we're still really good friends, but you know for me it was kind of this kind of idea that you know I was gonna stay married and there was kind of no chance for us and so it really was this kind of clandestine very like, um, really sexy affair. It reminded me so much of that movie with Richard Gere and Diane Laine called . . . uh, shit I forget the name of it; the one where she cheats on Richard Gere with a hot French lover. I think that particular movie does a very good job of encapsulating the feeling of the affair and starting off and the excitement and the thrill. . . . I mean to me it wasn't the tabooness of it, that wasn't appealing and I didn't like having to sneak around, but I knew that my husband couldn't handle it if I actually said, "Dude, I want to see other people." And I wanted to see other guys but I always kept it very separate and I was always very careful and very intentional to not have him find out. Because it was never vindictive. It was never about me wanting to hurt him; it was all about me wanting to get my needs met. And I felt that this was the way I was gonna handle it because I couldn't compromise my sexuality. That was a deal breaker for me in marriage and I thought this was the best way of handling it. I think it was what I knew how to do at the time.
>
> You know, I spent a lot of years compromising too much and now looking back I wish I would have just ended things sooner. He and I were both so unhappy. But I think that some of that emerged in the latter years of our marriage, that we really were just always missing each other and not always on that same page. And I have to believe that there was a reason I stayed. Other than grad school like, I was in the middle of my PhD. It was the worst time to get divorced. We had no money. You know, and we had kind of grown up together from twenty to thirty and I kind of feel like it sort of played itself out how it needed to. There is a part of me that feels like I missed out a little bit and there's another part of me that feels like I had some support during grad school when I think a lot of other people didn't. And so I think it's kind of like, I kind of wish that things would have been different and we kind of would have ended things sooner and

saved us both quite a bit of agony. Maybe that's what I needed to go through.

I think, I guess, I think I've had a couple of experiences since then and I've become much more aware after the work that I've done on fidelity and monogamous and non-monogamous relationships and I think the one thing I struggle most with is how to be this sort of agentic self and how to be yourself and how to be an individual and what that means when you are in a relationship, whether they be friendships or lovers or collegial or whatever. And one of the hardest things I really struggle with is that if there's somebody who asks me to be sexually or emotionally exclusive there's a need or desire that person has, just like I would do the same. And one of the things that I have yet to sort of reconcile is that the people that I choose to be with in my lifetime, whether those people are mine . . . are, I don't quite know how to say this. . . . This is sort of my life and my experience and I choose to maybe be with a partner and these satellite partners or experiences or whatever and I mean this is my way of experiencing the world and my sexuality and I think that one of the cool things about an affair is that the new relationship energy, I know the poly people talk about this a lot, and just the excitement of new that awakens the different part of who you are that awakens the parts that are dormant and just that inner connection that occurs when intimacy happens. For me it's usually sexual; I have a tendency not to get wrapped up emotionally in affairs but, you know, to like smell, you know the smells and the tastes and the newness of it is part of the thrill. And I think that the intention is also part of it too and I think that is what we are kind of struggling with in twenty-first-century sexuality. We are much more agentic and much more aware and much more individual and we kind of know more what we want than we ever have before especially as women and so . . . which is so exciting. But at the same time we have these very ancient dialogues and very archaic dialogues and scripts about sexuality about sexual pleasure and emotional pleasure and connectedness and even the word affair which I try to not be so cognizant about . . . just tell her what you experienced. I don't know I would probably use the word encounter or hook-ups or when it was emotional. . . . I don't know, I think affair is such a hard word for me. I was in love. I was in love with him for many, many years. Um, and um, so I think he was the closest thing to a traditional notion of an affair. It was emotional and sexual and the pining and the longing that comes with that so I would probably under most circumstances say affair um but I would probably call him my situation or I might I dunno. . . . I wish that I could give you a better word to use because it's . . . I don't even really like lover. Like how do I describe this person? You know? It was a connection that was aside from my life. And that's why an affair can be so powerful in the beginning stages. It's like excitement and fear all at once. Is this what I want? Can I want this? Should I want this? Wait. This feels so good. I'm not supposed to want this. What are the ramifications of this? What are the consequences? Can I do this on the side? Should I have this be the main event? You know? What is it like to have both? And so I think that those beginning stages for me . . . those are the things I thought most about and for me I kind of thought about my needs and it sounds so selfish today but back then I was at a point where I needed it and it was worth the consequences!

While phenomenological research demands a thorough reading of all the narratives (in this case forty-two of them), we will engage only a few more before proceeding to the next steps in analysis and the findings.

Another participant describes the narrowing of possibilities as he ages as an important backdrop for the time the affairs begin. He also describes profound feelings of sexual desire and rejection. Given that he wants to uphold his promise of monogamy as a model that is suitable for him, he feels desperate to have a sexually satisfying connection with his wife, who he perceives to be sexually dead and withholding. His understanding of the affair is that it stabilized the marriage by providing an outlet for his sexual needs so that he could otherwise maintain his monogamous relationship.

I am fifty-four years old and have been married to my wife for twenty years. It's my first marriage. We have a teenage daughter. I had my first affair about five years ago. Up until that point I had been entirely monogamous. Before I met my wife, I had been a serial monogamist. It has been a strong and meaningful structure for me.

What led to this affair was a long period of sexual frustration. To put it quite simply: I enjoy sex; my wife doesn't. We had a great sexual connection in the beginning. She was very open-minded, seductive and sexy. After a couple of months, however, I felt like an abrupt change occurred. The excitement was gone and I couldn't discern the reason. The frequency of our sexual encounters decreased and I remember concluding that she didn't love me anymore. Sex has been frustrating since those first few months essentially.

Over the years I have tried many things to address the issue. We talked a lot. I made it clear what I want. I asked about what she wanted. We read books, worked hard at creating opportunities for eroticism, tried various suggestions. Eventually I gave up. Every once in a while she would say, "I know you aren't happy. I'm not either." But then nothing changed. At some point I came to the conclusion that I can't seduce my wife. We ended up only having sex when she

wanted it (very infrequently) and how she wanted it (very rigidly
scripted). When I demonstrated any desire or creativity, she would
refuse. Eventually, I didn't try anymore. I found her attractive and yet
I felt so deeply rejected by her.

For many years I told myself to be patient, and thought that it
would get better. I figured we would rediscover our original connection perhaps when our daughter got older or some time had passed
or as she progressed through menopause and I told myself it would
be better then. Slowly my hopes faded. I didn't believe anymore
that anything would change. It had simply been too long and I felt
too badly about myself and deeply deprived and I didn't see a path
toward change as these events came to pass. I felt stuck in a sexless
marriage and felt confined. This was combined with a feeling of life
being too short to not have pleasure. I began to feel that I wanted to
not waste the next ten years of my life before I am too old to enjoy
anything anymore.

The woman I had my first affair with (of a total of two) was somebody I had known for more than ten years. She was attractive but
not somebody I would want a serious relationship with. Before we
had the affair she had been flirting with me for about two years. First
I felt like she wasn't serious or somehow didn't mean to address me
(my self-confidence was at a zero!). But she continued and made it
very clear what she wanted: Sex with me. There was no particular
incident I remember, that made me cross the line, I just did. At the
very beginning I felt very guilty and suffered from a bad conscience.
I almost couldn't do it on my first date with her. But then I had a
great time. She fulfilled so many wishes and yearnings I had had for
so many years. She loved to seduce, to dress up, to play, and to be
seduced. She complimented my body and gave me the feeling I was
really attractive, worthy, and sexy. What a treat after so many years
of frustration! This affair went on for almost two years (with some
breaks in between) and it was a wonderful time for me. In addition, she wasn't really looking for a serious relationship with me and
I wasn't more deeply interested in her. So in a way the affair stabilized my marriage and took some pressure off it.

Having the affair made me question my value system over and
over again, however. At the beginning I suffered from feeling guilty.
Then there was some aggression; my wife didn't deserve any better, because she rejected me so, I reasoned. Then I sometimes felt
like I sort of wanted her to find out about the affair so that she
might understand just how dramatically she had impacted me. Then
I just thought, "Just fuck the values, life is short and I want to enjoy
myself." Then, maybe I thought I should adapt my values. I still think
that it is almost impossible to meet all your needs in a monogamous

relationship. Now I have two conflicting values: Fidelity to my wife and fidelity to myself. These two are still somewhat at odds. We are in couples counseling working on these issues now.

There are many more narratives in this data set, each with their accompanying details and context. As noted earlier, phenomenological research requires that we move from the particular details to the abstraction of these details so as to reveal the structure of the narratives that might describe the essence of the beginning of an affair shared across narratives. The challenge in research of this nature is to consider if there are constituents that are common across the abstracted narratives that hang together and support one another as a structural description that if altered would produce a different phenomenon or experience and to be critical with any early attempts at understanding. This process includes transforming each narrative into an abstracted set of essential statements that are descriptive and that neither add nor subtract any essential meanings. Thereafter commonalities are considered and imaginative variation of details is employed.

In the forty-two narratives, there was sufficient commonality between the transformed narratives as a whole to present a single structure of the experience of infidelity from the perspective of the person who engages in it. After applying the method described in chapter 4 to these descriptions and considering if any of the proposed constituents would, if not included, define a different experience than that of beginning an instance of infidelity, what follows remains.

The Essential Structure of the Beginning of Infidelity

The beginning of an affair or an instance of infidelity occurs against the backdrop of a relationship that feels unsatisfactory, sorely lacking in fundamental and critically important ways, and hopeless to improve, from the perspective of the person who begins an affair. The areas that are experienced as lacking include intimacy, novelty, passion, and/or sexual satisfaction. This is viewed as a problem that has no possible solution to the person who experiences it; it is a dilemma. The persistent and unchallenged view remains that it is hopeless to talk about it with the partner and further that it is the partner who could change to alleviate the problem and is somehow also unable and/or unwilling to do so. The view of the one who begins the affair is that he or she has an appetite and appreciation that is inherently greater than that of the partner for novelty, passion, connection, and sexual adventure in sexual and romantic relationships. The one who begins the affair views the self as a good partner who has an intact sense of desire and has navigated this conflict well (e.g. having tried to improve the situation and remaining loyal despite the challenges of having what are viewed as appropriate and healthy desires that remain unmet) and the partner is viewed as bad (e.g. withholding, willful, boring, deficient, or/and lacking sexual vitality), and these are understood as fixed and inherent characteristics of the partner. With this view of the self as good and the other as bad, and both as fixed and unchangeable, the one who begins an affair also experiences the self as deserving of passion, novelty, and sexual satisfaction—hopeless to achieve this within the primary relationship.

At the same time, there is largely a lack of curiosity about the partner—what the partner may want, feel, deserve, or experience—or what the consequences may be for them with this set of constituents. The partner is not fully animated as a subject in the mind of the one who begins an affair in part because he or she is perceived as fixed and bad and predictably so. No novel experiences in the realm of sexuality, eroticism, or intimacy are thought to be possible to arise from this other and therefore the hopelessness and lack of curiosity seems justified. While the one who has the affair acknowledges that the situation is stuck and unsatisfying, divorce/breaking up or opening up the relationship are interestingly not considered in earnest as possible options for solving the dilemma, as this would conflict with the fixed view of the self as a good partner who is loyal; the structure of an affair necessitates the lack of realistic consideration of a structural solution changing the commitment. The primary relationship continues in an unsatisfying fashion with little motivation or attempt to change it or improve it and no path to resolve what is perceived as hopeless.

The beginning of an affair then occurs as the one who begins an affair meets someone outside of the relationship and experiences the self, compelled by curiosity and interest toward another, who is also reciprocally curious and interested about the one who begins an affair. This mutual interest is not necessarily understood as erotic or sexual at the particular moment in time of the first meeting, although it can be, nor is there a clear sense of this becoming a potential affair at the moment that interest is registered. Instead there is a reciprocal reinforcing sense of curiosity and interest that deepens and develops the connection over some measure of time, fueling each other into further escalating interest, until a point when the two experience eroticism or passion in an act that has sexual significance. This recognition of interest, or the recognition of a sexual atmosphere, can take moments or years and is not experienced as a choice or a decision that occurs at a particular moment in time, even though there are clearly choices that the one who begins an affair makes to facilitate the possibility of mutual reciprocal interest developing over time. The process is experienced as a particular set of feelings (e.g. passion, novelty, interest, deserving) overriding judgment. The moment the experience is recognized and named as erotic, passionate, and/or sexual generally occurs through reflection with hindsight on a moment of a clear and undeniable active and sexual and/or intimate line is crossed for the one who begins the affair. In retrospect, however, there is a reflection and recognition of the many small actions that the one who begins the affair actively willfully participates in that occurred prior to the moment of recognition of the affair, to facilitate the development of the affair that can be categorized as erotic or flirtatious. There is also a reflection after the fact that the primary relationship was headed toward crisis or a break-up all along. The beginning of an affair is lived pre-egoically, in an embodied manner, and similarly the marriage is headed toward divorce, also lived pre-egoically, in an embodied manner, and is the backdrop against which the affair develops. Only once this eroticism is noticed, and therefore the acts that allowed it to build, is there guilt and concern about the affair in some form.

We cannot say that this is the *universal* essence of an affair because there are possibilities of infidelities that we can imagine or have heard of or experienced that can fall outside of this description—for example those who pre-plan affairs and seek them out deliberately (although those might better describe the essence of a hook-up), or those who are not particularly dissatisfied but seek them out in addition to their primary relationship, for example (and I might also call these instances cases of poly-oriented persons needing to come out because people who can truly love and be satisfied with more than one relationship are more in line with the polyamory position, rather than those who are engaging in infidelities). Obviously there are many more possibilities than those described earlier. The burden of drawing the line somewhere on what exactly we are aiming to describe in order to articulate 1) a structure that is essential, 2) hangs together as one structure, and 3) gets to the heart of the issue—infidelity—is important in these forty-two stories. Deliberate hook-ups or lack of dissatisfaction were simply not present in the data; therefore we conclude that the more general psychological phenomenon includes dissatisfaction and a pre-egoic recognition of the infidelity. What follows then is a discussion of how these data support the structure and why each constituent part is important in defining the structure.

Explication of Constituents

In phenomenological research, the resulting descriptive structure is provided as a whole. However, it is also comprised of constituent parts that reinforce one another. I have provided discussion of how each supports the larger structure as a whole in this section.

The constituents of the structure are as follows:

1. Dissatisfaction and hopelessness in the relationship.
2. A value of novelty and passion in romantic/sexual relationships.
3. A sense of deserving sexual satisfaction and intimate connection.
4. The partner and self are viewed as fixed characters.
5. Lack of curiosity for the partner as a subject.
6. An experience of desire and passion overriding and overtaking one's judgment.
7. The affair is not recognized as an affair until after it begins.
8. Divorce or opening up the relationship are not considered options for resolving the issues.

These eight constituents are derived from the descriptions collected, and each structurally supports the essence of the development of an affair in that if one or more are not present, the entire experience would be better described as something other than the experience of beginning an affair. For example, if one is dissatisfied and feels entitled to satisfying sex but is also curious about the partner's experience or he or she seems to not be a fixed character but instead is capable of change, this describes a case where counseling is more likely to be pursued, or additional endeavoring for improvement will occur and the infidelity will be less likely. If divorce or opening up are considered in earnest, an affair is not necessary. If one does not experience desire overriding judgment but instead considers an affair more directly before it occurs, perhaps this pierces the idea that one is a good partner more directly, and one is more directly confronted with the dilemma and is less likely to go forward with the act itself. It is this mutual structural reinforcing quality of the constituents that makes them essential in phenomenological analyses. It is also these constituents that can become points of intervention in a clinical approach to infidelity and its sequelae, discussed more fully in chapter 6. It becomes important to consider possibilities for changing one or more of the structural components to make conscious the decision-points in relationships.

The following excerpts and discussion of the content from interviews illustrate the basis for the constituents and structure. Not all of the text from each narrative will be presented here; it is too voluminous. Excerpts that have been anonymized by altering identifying information to protect confidentiality are provided to illustrate each and are examples of how the abstractions to the larger structure were made.

1. Dissatisfaction and Hopelessness in the Relationship

While all of the participants focused largely on describing the events and experiences leading to the beginning of the affair, all of them also described their primary relationships at the time of the affair in contrast, even it if was only one small side note. While it may not be surprising that their primary relationships were unsatisfactory in some ways or that this is a way that they might frame their relationships at the time of an experience they consider to be an instance of infidelity, there are two important issues to consider that are made clear through the structure. First, the affair for these participants appears to be lived in a manner that underscores its existence *in contrast to* the primary relationship, not in a manner that is experienced as an event that occurs *in addition to* or *aside from* the relationship. Some descriptions include an attempt to live the affairs aside from the relationship, and yet there is always a fair amount of description (unprompted) dedicated to the hopelessness for satisfaction within the primary relationship as contrasted to the experiences within the infidelity.

Second, the dissatisfaction with the primary relationship is coupled with a resignation to a level of hopelessness and despair that is marked and that forecloses any further effort to improve the primary relationship and represents a lack of vitality leading to the sense of deserving and lack of curiosity for the partner. This suggests that people who begin affairs may also be subscribing to the belief that both satisfaction and dissatisfaction within a relationship is due to inherent qualities of the people who make up the couple and not contextual issues or dynamics between couples that affect couples or perceptions that can shift and change. In addition, it also suggests that there is some amount of effort that people are willing to do but that there are moments in time when a decision is made to stop all efforts and to give up trying. This particular moment for a couple is an interesting one, as it is a decision that changes the nature of how the future of the couple is experienced and often is made unilaterally and sometimes without what a couples therapist might suggest is needed. Sometimes this particular decision is about sexuality (e.g. types of sex acts, frequency of sex, passion) and other times it is about the hopelessness of communicating or connecting with the partner intimately at all. The giving up is also supported by the belief that there is no use talking about the issues and further that nothing can change. This belief tends to prevent couples from seeking outside help as well, thus cementing the fixed beliefs because no new information enters the system.

The extent of the dissatisfaction and hopelessness is illustrated in a few excerpts.

> "I'd already been really unhappy . . . like our sex life was nonexistent. . . . I was sick of waiting around for this to happen. . . . I realized how much I missed sex and how much I missed intimacy and physical connection . . . we went for counseling for awhile . . . and there was no chance for us."

"My relationship with my wife was damaged. We had certainly reached an impasse."

"Slowly my hope faded. I didn't believe anymore that things would change. I felt stuck in a more or less sexless marriage."

"She just couldn't be a good wife at the same time for me. She left the building when it came to taking care of our life."

"At that point in my relationship with my partner it was a frickin' minefield. I didn't need to give her any ammunition. Uh, we were not getting along at all. It was constant push and pull navigation to just try to get along."

"At the time I was in an unhappy, asexual marriage."

2. A Value of Novelty and Passion in Romantic/Sexual Relationships

An important similarity between the participants' descriptions was a perceived discrepancy between their descriptions of themselves and their spouses in terms of appetite or desire for passion and novelty and a strong value placed upon novelty and passion in love and sex that is viewed as a critical ingredient required of a good relationship, giving rise to the dissatisfaction and hopelessness when it is not present. The descriptions include sensuous language of romance, eroticism, and vitality that were present in the discussions of the affairs in contrast to those of the primary relationships. The focus was notably not on other aspects of love relationships that could have been mentioned, such as familiarity, constancy, safety, and reliability. The focus was also not necessarily on particular sexual behaviors or acts but rather was more clearly related to the less concrete experiences of desire, or an atmosphere of eroticism and passion. What this suggests is that affairs occur in the midst of unmet desire, when romance, playfulness, and sensuousness are lacking, having little to do with lack of mechanical sexual skills or particular sexual acts and behaviors. In some cases people also mention fantasy as being important to their motivations.

One participant describes his feelings as the affair developed:

"It was very kind of romantic and hot and sweet and all that and I started comparing it to my existing relationship which was maybe six or six and a half years old and a very different vibe. And so yeah, the chemistry is just completely different. And so all of a sudden I was looking at my marriage differently. Like there are some things which are lacking; my wife isn't paying attention to me or whatever. . . . I was wrapped up in J. I was writing poetry about J and all that. I really loved the allure of someone else having that kind of attraction to me and I was having it too for her."

Another describes the beginning of the affair in a way that makes it clear how much novelty and vitality was available after crossing the line. She notes: "The kiss was like opening a huge door into another land." This is also contrasted later in her narrative with descriptions of abuse and lack of excitement and intimacy in the relationship.

Another focuses on the issue of variety and passion quite directly and links this to a spiritual sensibility:

> "I recall an underlying sense of guilt and . . . I was very close to losing all of my dignity and pride . . . then I felt wild, uninhibited and free with her . . . fucking a different kind of pussy was alluring to me. She was spiritual. My partner was material."

3. A Sense of Deserving Sexual Satisfaction or Intimate Connection

In addition to wanting passion and novelty and seeing them as critical elements of romantic love and partnership, these participants take this further to a sense of deserving or entitlement. Sexuality, experienced in a novel and passionate manner, is experienced as critical to the self, part of the participants' identities, something that cannot be denied or forsaken, and something that has been ignored or not present for a long time in their monogamous relationships. The urgency to have passion, and the feeling of deservingness, is related to the passage of time, both how long it has been and how much longer they can tolerate a passionless relationship.

One participant notes: "I have always been such a sexual person and . . . he wasn't in a place to handle who I was sexually." She later describes, "I was just like, fuck it man, I am sick of like waiting around for this to happen and this just feels so good."

Another says that the affair occurred because of the chronicity of his disappointment with his partner and her lack of availability to him. He felt he deserved attention:

> "My partner had agreed to go with me to the conference. I was in an emotional free fall that she backed out at the last minute to be with her parents. The in-laws were a chronic problem in our relationship. She was more a daughter to them than a partner to me."

Another participant recalls how long her suffering had gone on before she describes the beginning of her affair.

> "I was totally miserable and let's see I was in my early thirties and um fell out of love with my husband on the honeymoon when I was

seventeen. He was an alcoholic and a womanizer and so year after year, I raised two little girls pretty much by myself and became more miserable, more vacuous, and he was a wham bam thank you ma'am kind of lover—no fulfilling sex whatsoever—and the emotional connection was on every level. . . . I was prime for an affair."

One participant really linked the issue to existential questions:

"I became more and more conscious that my lifetime is confined. When I was around forty-five more and more of my friends and acquaintances began to suffer with serious diseases and issues. . . . So me having an affair was about me being a person who loves passionate sex, combined with a great frustration about my sex life in my marriage, the realization that things were getting worse instead of better, no idea how I could turn things around."

4. The Partner and Self Are Viewed as Fixed Characters

Both the self and the partner are viewed by the one who begins the affair as unwilling and/or incapable of change on particular dimensions that are thought to be important to a satisfying relationship. This is attributed to the perception of inherently fixed capacities in the self and other related to sexuality, eroticism, passion, romance, and novelty. These capacities are considered intact in the self but insufficiently developed in the other. This view is particularly important because it does not allow for an alternative understanding of the experience as being a relational phenomenon, or related to contextual factors or to changeable aspects of the self or other. It also does not account for the view that perhaps the other has a set of capacities and desires that are equally intact. Choice or developmental aspects are not prominent considerations with respect to how these capacities or proclivities might shift over time. Further, the participant holds another set of fixed views of the self and other that includes a moral character judgment. The self is viewed as a good partner and the partner is viewed as a bad one. This is reasoned due to the fact that the partner does not appear to have sexual or erotic desires or does not act on them within the sanctioned structure of monogamy, where these are viewed that they should be, and therefore is perceived as having deliberately and punitively withheld love or affection or/and as being sexually or erotically deficient. This particular set of judgments makes an explanation possible—a defensible narrative that explains why cheating, which is viewed as morally wrong by the participants, is in their case justifiable. The entitlement to sexual satisfaction and the perception of fixedness of the characters create the necessary ingredients upon which it is possible to justify the acts that allow the participant to do what they also deem is bad behavior or morally objectionable behavior in the abstract. This suggests that the situated experience of engaging in infidelity allows an alternative ethical narrative. This also suggests that research based on evaluation of hypothetical scenarios is significantly problematic.

One participant describes his wife and himself, who had an open relationship, as inherently different in terms of their respective abilities to separate sex and love. He suggests that these differences are fixed and unchangeable with respect to how they approach the open structure they have negotiated. He adds that it is not the sexual openness that is the problem for them but rather the impact on their connection that became problematic. He notes:

> "She really fell in love with somebody. And that was a real threat and I forced that to shut down once they fell in love. Because it really started . . . M said she could handle it and be a good wife. She could be in love with two people (laughs) and quite honestly, M COULD have been in love with two people. She just couldn't be a good wife at the same time for ME. And she left the building when it came to taking care of our life!"

Another participant describes very different approaches to sexuality and eroticism and locates these as inherent qualities in herself and her husband:

> "I am a pretty passionate person and very sexual person and . . . he was a wham bam thank you ma'am."

Another participant describes himself as a fixed character:

> "I love passion, and you know, I love beauty, and hey, the whole incipient affair in the parlance of our time is just full of that stuff. . . . I'm easily bored by people. . . . I'm a very curious person who experiences a lot but I find that people . . . you know there's a monotony to a relationship with anybody."

Another characterizes his partner as lacking desire, arousal, and responsiveness:

> "My wife is asexual. No interest in sex (other than avoiding it) and no physical response to any kind of stimulation. Yet she is also extremely possessive."

One feels angry and hopeless about a particular dynamic and finds the character of their partner problematic. This makes it possible to justify how the partner is bad and the self is good—and why an affair is possible:

> "Does she ever take responsibility for anything? No. Ugh. It was a huge fight and I was just so fucking pissed off at her and so by the first night (on my trip away from her) I was like, 'Fuck her!'"

5. Lack of Curiosity for the Partner as a Subject

These participants all seemed to be largely concerned with the self in their narratives, and there was a general lack of curiosity about the partner's experience or subjectivity. This is demonstrated in the ways that the participants do not give much attention or consideration to the potential feelings and thoughts of the partner in the descriptions of the beginning of an affair. This is supported by the view of the self and partner as fixed, which forecloses further curiosity about the possibilities of vitality within the partner. The partner is viewed as predictable and in this case predictably deficient, withholding, and unsatisfactory. This lack of curiosity allows for relatively little reflection in the descriptions on the promise of monogamy and the subsequent betrayal as it could be perceived or experienced by the partner, nor the possibility that the partner may be equally unhappy in the marriage for the same or different reasons.

This is illustrated by one participant considering that the partner has a self but also her inability to consider the subjectivity of the partner much more: "I kind of wasn't in a place to handle what he needed." The remainder of her description includes a discussion of her unmet physical and emotional needs but does not include any further reflection on how her unmet needs were received by him and what this implies about her responsibilities in the discussion: How he might feel similarly hopeless and unhappy having unmet needs or how his needs might be met in the current arrangement or what his needs were specifically. Further, there was no discussion or reflection on the idea that perhaps "meeting needs" might not be the only way to evaluate the quality of their relationship and that perhaps he might have a different set of criteria for satisfaction.

Another participant notes that his desire to experience passion and novelty was stronger than any obligation he may have felt to consider the implications for his wife's desires, needs, and feelings. "You know I would essentially do anything I needed to, which meant upsetting my wife, um . . . but that bothered me less than needing to be around [the other woman]."

Another only considers her partner so much to state that he was horrible and there is no further reflection on his perspective or the impact her affair may have on him. She felt justified. She notes: "And so that led to me doing things that I never thought I'd be doing. . . . That was the beginning of the end of my loyalty to this kind of . . . pretty horrible man."

One participant, due to ongoing frustration, begins an affair. His consideration of his partner is only cursory in that he thinks about how she might react to him if he is caught while he makes out with this woman he has met. He doesn't consider how she may feel or what this act may mean for their relationship in a larger sense, however; instead he feels entitled to cheat because she flirts unabashedly with others.

> "She does shit like this all the time. For one thing, she is the queen of the double standard. She wasn't there so of course she's gonna say, 'The minute I'm not there of course you are making out with somebody!' "

6. An Experience of Desire Overtaking and Overriding one's Judgment

The participants describe the relationship with the person with whom they begin an affair and the events leading up to the moment they recognize the experience and they name it an affair. This recognition is bound together with naming the experience as a passionate or sexual experience as separate from a socially sanctioned one from the perspective of the monogamous commitment. This also makes clear that it may be more difficult to recognize and name an emotional affair "an affair" as it develops because the passion and sexuality may not be as prominent in the experience. Passion and sexual significance are recognized the moment that there is an embodied act that is accomplished through space and time; it is not a cognitive act or a fantasy that marks the line being crossed in these narratives. Although theoretically with the definition of perceived betrayals discussed in chapters 1 and 2, the experiences of fantasies and emotional affairs can be implicated and for some are considered problematic. With hindsight, most participants are able to consider the acts that led up to the moment they recognized the affair, including instances of flirtation and clear decisions and actions they took that helped make the affair possible. As it was being lived, however, the significance of these acts and decisions was not clear to them.

At the particular moment that each recognizes the sexually embodied act that is crossing the line, they also describe themselves as somewhat passive, but willing, participants in the acts. These are acts that the one who begins an affair desires, consents to, and participates in (sometimes even orchestrates), but they are described as if they are *happening to* the participant, as if he or she is an object of a powerful outside (pleasurable and sensory-rich) force, rather than an experience that is volitional and directed with agency, as a conscious subject. There is a transcendent quality of the self, a giving over to a larger force outside of the self and other—a quality of destiny to the experience.

For one participant, the moment of transgression is described as: "We *ended up* having sex." While she offers a subject for this sentence, "we" and, in doing so, implicates both herself and her lover as subjects in these acts, the rest of the sentence, "ended up," implies a sense of participating in the moment-to-moment activities that presumably led to sex (e.g. foreplay, intimate touch, or at the very least removal or pushing aside clothing) in an organic way. "Ended up" implies being overtaken by an outside force without much thought, planning, or intention, demonstrating abandon to what is later described as "passion in the moment." This also somewhat deflects responsibility for the acts and reflects the ways in which affairs come into being in a pre-egoic manner.

In another case, there is a sense of an outside force that comes to dominate the participant's experience altogether in a moment, somewhat like Cupid's arrow. One participant notes: "I was smitten." While there is a subject "I" and a transformation has taken place in his narrative from observing her and being interested and curious, to feeling something much stronger, he implies that he is overtaken by the power of a force in that instant and he does not locate that power in his gaze, thoughts, intentions, or actions to create such a feeling. Further he also does not credit her beauty or allure with this power. He has in this instant become part of a larger powerful outside force that animates this moment for both of them in a mythic manner, and he uses the passive voice to describe this. Again, this somewhat deflects responsibility and control for the outcome of the events.

Another person states: "There was a kiss." She does not discuss who initiated it and presumably it was an effortless smooth motor choreography that occurred without much discussion or planning, like a handshake or inviting someone into the house with a gesture. She does not focus on the subjects in the act and their movements; the kiss occurs romantically and opens the door to another land for her. This is the only sentence that does not include pronouns in her description. And yet one could argue that she is a subject (as is her lover) in this kiss with culpability and choice to engage or not. One can also surmise that there were gestures (e.g. leaning toward the other) that made the kiss possible. This particular statement reflects the ideas in Merleau-Ponty's discussion of the importance of gesture in creating a sexual atmosphere and also in the possibility that gesture is the mechanism through which eroticism can be communicated without much conscious decision-making or discussion.

One participant describes a feeling of passion overcoming him and influencing a decision to accept a very direct offer to have sex. He says, "I was propositioned by a friend to have sex without my partner. I felt an underlying sense of guilt and that I was close to losing my dignity but then a lion's roar kind of feeling of passion came." While he did accept the offer and therefore did decide to betray his partner, he blames the felt sense of passion for his actions that came to him. He does not locate this feeling as generating from a conscious intentional place; it is rather something that happened to him.

Another participant describes how the allure of the woman he eventually has an affair with just takes over; it is a feeling that replaces judgment and he only realizes that he has been moved into action bypassing the moment of deciding later. He finds himself fantasizing and compelled to be with her, and that force develops the affair. He writes,

> "So I just started getting taken over by the experience of J, that's her name. And I just created this fantasy world, which wasn't real but it was a fun little world to live in. And it was you know, there was no physical contact for the first year of this, but I was wrapped up in J."

Another does not assign agency or intention directly, although he implies that she initiated contact by approaching him at his table. He avoids discussing any role that he directly had in forwarding the agenda to have sex with her, and yet he implies that he participated willingly. He describes: "I was sitting alone and a female approached me to talk. We had two drinks and went upstairs to my room. The time was glorious!" Ostensibly, he invited her to the room, used his key to get into the room, and so on, but these parts of the description are only logically implied. He assigns her the role of agent in approaching him, but his role is passive. He is overtaken by the situation—compelled to act through gesture, not a cognitive decision-making process.

A passivity occurs in these stories where one is carried away by the passion and excitement of the moment, which are not narrated with agentic details. It could also be that the participants use the passive voice or implied agency without being direct in order to avoid responsibility or shame for their actions. This constituent demonstrates passive intentionality that occurs in the moment of crossing the line. It also illustrates the ways we tend to romanticize sexual and erotic engagements and how little control or agency we feel we have at times. This will become important for treatment planning directions I discuss in the subsequent chapters.

7. The Affair Is Not Recognized as an Affair Until After It Begins

The participants do not describe scenarios in which they cognitively contemplate or choose actively to have an affair. There is no moment of deciding in the way other types of decisions are met (e.g. choosing a college, deciding to trade in a car, deciding to hire a new assistant). Similarly, they do not experience the affair as a biological imperative even though there is yearning, entitlement, and physical response. In each description, there is a retrospective understanding that many more of the events leading up to the moment they named the experience infidelity could be considered part of the affair, but that at the time it was occurring and developing it was not understood as sexual, erotic, or an instance of infidelity, until particular actions occurred that were understood as sexual and concrete and undeniable from the perspective of the person who began the affair. Prior to this point, each participant had been living the infidelity pre-egoically. And at the moment it is grasped consciously and named an affair for the participants, the people engaging in these experiences become subjects in the act of having an affair and are thus returned to the state of consciousness where they more clearly understand culpability or at least the implications of the act.

For one participant, the affair had been developing, but then all at once it became clear that it had already occurred. He says:

> "I just remember we had a conversation where it started out as a heartfelt conversation about something, I don't even remember what and all of a sudden, the sexy started coming on. I was really attracted to her and she was really attracted to me and we hadn't even kissed. We were lightly touching and that's when the floor dropped on the safety of that relationship. We fell into something deep and sexy and it was completely different from then on. I thought about her non-stop for days and days. And you know emailed back and forth and she felt the same. . . . But at the same time what made it an illicit affair was not that my wife didn't know but that I was really checked out at times with somebody else, spending a lot more time thinking about her and not my wife for days on end."

Another describes the moment of crossing the line from two friends having a coffee to an affair as follows:

> "He said, 'Would you like to go have coffee?' and it was like 8 o'clock and I went and by that time I was very attracted to him and we went and had coffee, a two-hour coffee. There was a coffee shop across the street and he walked me to the parking ramp; there was a kiss and that was . . . the straw that broke the camel's back. . . . The kiss was like opening a huge door into another land . . . and that led me to doing things that I never thought I'd be doing, like flying to other cities."

Another describes the passive way that he drifts into an affair:

> "Gradually we drifted from teacher/student, to friends to lovers and then to spouses."

What is interesting here is that he discusses the beginning of an affair but does not attribute intentionality or direct agency to himself, his lover, or his former spouse. He similarly passively describes the sequence toward the affair and divorce.

8. Divorce or Opening Up the Relationship Are Not Considered Real Options

Given the level of hopelessness and dissatisfaction, belief that the partner and self are fixed characters, and that one is deserving of sexual satisfaction, it is only logical that one might consider divorce, or the possibility of opening up the marriage as potential solutions to the perceived dilemma. These participants, however, give these ideas very little consideration in their narratives, or if they do, they generally dismiss these as possible options without much consideration. This is one of the reasons that infidelity occurs; there is no consideration of possible structural solutions nor is there a discussion of the seriousness of the dilemma contrasted with these structural options. It is as if the person experiencing the affair has already decided that they are in significant crisis and that they cannot discuss this with their partner in great depth. Often the partner does not know of the extent of upset and disconnection, yet discussions of opening up or divorce would have facilitated this understanding and helped the couple to evaluate the extent of the issues. The affair is partially designed to make possible living with a secret—that there is significant disappointment with the primary relationship. We tend to focus on the secret affair, and yet in all of these instances the failure to discuss the depth of disappointment and frustration effectively is also a secret.

One woman considers divorce in retrospect. (They ended up divorced eventually.) She says, "You know I spent a lot of years compromising too much and now looking back I wish I would have just ended things sooner. He and I were both so unhappy. . . . But it was the worst time to get divorced!" She also mentions that he would not be interested in a non-monogamous situation. "I knew that he couldn't handle it if I actually said . . . 'I want to see other people.'" She never ended up asking.

Many participants had practical considerations making divorce a more difficult option. Many cited the potential financial impact as problematic. "I would have likely gotten a divorce but . . . I had to make enough to support two daughters by myself," said one participant. This particular constituent represents an instance of, according to the participants, retrospectively recognizing that there was an inevitability of trending toward a divorce that was already being lived and was present to them but that there were risks associated with changing the structure of the primary relationship. With the beginning of the affair, which is marked by the moment in time when the infidelity is recognized and named as such, after a sexually signifying act, a marriage trending toward divorce is also grasped and recognized by these participants.

As noted earlier, several people mentioned that the affair stabilized their marriages by providing satisfying sex so that the rest of the marriage could remain intact without conflict. "Because my wife had no interest in sex and was also extremely jealous at the idea of opening up our relationship, an affair that was secret was my answer." Interestingly, this person did not consider divorce, since this particular stabilizing solution worked for him and allowed the conflict within him to subside.

Many felt that open relationships, while compelling theoretically, were problematic and would be difficult for them to manage and as a result preferred to have an affair.

One describes his feelings about open relationships in great detail:

"I'm not a very monogamous kind of person. It's not a very natural state for me. . . . I'm pretty bad at it and it's easy for me to, you know, form strong relationships with people and in particular women. Unfortunately I haven't set up my relationships as open relationships because I would probably, you know, that's relatively rare in my generation. I'm sure it's hard and there's aggravation back and forth but I would be better off that way or not getting into exclusive relationships. I mean that's paradoxical because I'm also extremely domestic. I mean even though in the long run I am not really. . . . At the end of the day I think I'd rather not cohabitate and I think I'd rather not have exclusive relationships and it's hard to do because I like to have real relationships and it's hard to not get to the point where people are seeking commitment. . . . You know, I love intimacy. If you are gonna get intimacy, you are gonna have relationships and if you are gonna have relationships, you are gonna have . . . you are subject to domesticity and dailyness. . . . I think I would be ok with my partners having affairs. I mean I'm not very jealous. I think I mean I would be the kind of person who could thrive in an open relationship. I haven't tried it. I don't know if that's true. It may be an illusion. It might be awful if I wasn't getting any. Often that's the situation; it's bad because one person is off having fun and the other person is dealing with whatever in the nest and domestic relations or just the fact that so-and-so doesn't love me anymore and I feel like crap."

These eight constituents are the essential structural elements present for those who engage in infidelity. Because they are put forth in a descriptive manner gleaned from within the phenomenological attitude, they are not attached to a particular clinical theory and can be applied in a broad manner to clinical work, either through using them directly within a humanistic stance or through viewing them through the lens of any clinical framework as an interpretive second step. However, in the discussions in the next two chapters, I argue for a more flexible application than any particular interpretative framework and offer suggested approaches to cases of infidelity informed by this analysis that privileges the lived experience of those who have affairs and uses each constituent. I also argue for an approach that more directly confronts the experience of the one who has the affair rather than the couple or one who has been betrayed, both of which are more typically the focus in clinical work.

Part II

Chapter 6

Clinical Treatment Directions

In the previous chapters, I illustrated that there is little agreement among clinicians on how to best approach infidelity treatment. Many clinicians describe these cases as particularly difficult. This is for many reasons: The often explosive or intense emotions felt by clients, the secrecy and shame felt by the one who had the affair in particular, and the confusion about how something like this could have occurred to people who otherwise consider themselves to be ethical and good partners. All of these forces conspire to make it challenging for the one who had the affair to feel comfortable with a full authentic disclosure and exploration of feelings in psychotherapy or couples counseling. As a result, the treatment is often skewed toward addressing the needs of the person who was betrayed (especially in couples formats), and perhaps rightfully so, as this person is usually experiencing tremendous upset and these feelings are almost always very accessible and socially sanctioned. Often the treatment does not deepen later, however, to include full exploration of the rest of the feelings and dynamics that may underlie the infidelity for either partner.

It is also difficult to develop agreement on treatment goals that all parties share, including the therapist, because of the reasons stated earlier. Sometimes even the unit of treatment (couple, individual, or both) is not clear to the clinician at the outset, and multiple layers of iterative assessment are needed to consider the role of sexuality concerns, attachment issues, personality considerations, substance use, problems with technology use, and relational dynamics along the way. In addition, research shows that there is often a series of unexamined assumptions on the part of the clinician that leads to biases in treatment planning. Recall that clinicians have been found to hold biases toward whatever circumstances or relationship structures have been personally positive for them (e.g. monogamy, divorce, open relationships). As a result they often default to the implicit goal of what was favorable personally rather than to consider what might be in the clients' best interests. For all these reasons there is a need to consider anew treatment directions for infidelity.

The phenomenological structure discussed earlier, gleaned from research among those who have had affairs after promising monogamy, forms the basis of the new proposed treatment direction. I selected the perspective of the one who had the affair for research, which will drive the treatment model presented in this chapter because this is the viewpoint that I have found most lacking in both research and clinical discussions thus far. It is also the viewpoint that is least likely to be addressed in couples therapy and is a viewpoint that is more often than not judged by clinicians and society alike. Further, the underlying concerns that preceded the affair described in the phenomenological structure are usually most acutely felt by the one who has the affair and often remain unstated or understated unless the perspective of the person who had the affair is directly addressed. The idea embedded within this suggested new direction is that providing a non-judgmental but curious client-centered exploration of the infidelity in a more balanced manner (e.g. considering the perspectives of both parties deeply) will help those who have had affairs to give voice to their concerns more fully and to transform the forces that made the affairs possible. I hypothesize that these same concerns are what will, if voiced and explored, make authentic intimacy and connection more possible in their relationships or make clear a more conscious and complete decision about how to move forward. This is contrasted to the usual views that apology and forgiveness are what will result in renewed trust and therefore intimacy and connection. The perspective of the model I present here is that apology and forgiveness and therefore trust will not be complete or sufficient if the feelings that lie beneath the affair and that potentiated the affair are not also explored.

In order to make clear the relationship between authenticity and intimacy that I am embracing, it is important to discuss the meaning of intimacy first. For many, the word intimacy implies sexual intimacy and is associated with positive feelings and experiences of closeness. It is a warm and fuzzy feeling that we use to describe being close to another. It could also, however in contrast be intimate to share personal details or feelings that are largely difficult and that may result in conflicts or upset. This is another aspect of closeness—authentic sharing—and may result in warm fuzzy feelings, more challenging emotional experiences, or distance. Underlying and preceding the affairs within these narratives is in all cases a discussion of the difficulty in sharing fully and truthfully the extent of the issues and disappointments felt by the partner who has the affair within the primary relationship. The magnitude of suffering is not shared, or not in sufficient detail to impact the partner. The beginning of the split or secrecy that makes the affair possible has its roots in the lack of shared understanding of the extent of the dissatisfaction. Sometimes partners withhold (consciously or otherwise) particular wishes or fantasies, and other times it is the anger and loneliness or other difficult feelings that are withheld. Treatment, therefore, should also include developing the relationship so as to contain and make space for difficult intimate sharing of feelings and perspectives including desires—and the requisite emotion tolerance skills and differentiation required to do so. This is best done when there is, at some point in the therapy, a focus on the perspective and feelings of the one who engaged in infidelity: In particular an examination of what underlies this experience and a facilitated discussion with the couple to process these feelings. This differs from an apology and also from a discussion designed to facilitate closeness and warm fuzzy feelings of intimacy that so many couples counselors seem to privilege.

As we move toward treatment planning discussions, I offer one caveat that is important to reiterate. Infidelity is not a diagnosis with a set of concrete descriptive criteria and an agreed-upon etiology, even though there is an underlying structure I presented earlier. It can be experienced in a great variety of ways and may imply different meanings for each client. Treatment for infidelity is therefore a suggested set of directions and considerations rather than a manualized process that addresses concrete symptoms with an agreed-upon treatment goal. However, there are some similarities across cases of infidelity. I will use these similarities to develop the treatment directions in what follows and will focus on the perspective of the person who had the affair. The usual clinical skills and considerations, such as assessment for comorbid conditions as one might find in the DSM-V (APA, 2013), still applies to cases of infidelity alongside what is offered in this text. Some of these are rehashed in this chapter, albeit in a cursory manner, to make clear for early career clinicians how one might step-by-step consider the early treatment planning. Later, integration of the phenomenological findings is provided. In addition, areas in which clinicians do not receive adequate training, such as sexuality concerns and problematic technology use, but that nevertheless often co-occur with infidelity, also require assessment and consideration and do not appear in the DSM-V (APA, 2013) and are discussed. In addition, there is no agreement on their etiology or symptom presentations making treatment planning more artful than other clinically well-understood phenomena. All of these dimensions are addressed in the framework presented in this chapter.

Beginning Treatment and Creating a Therapeutic Alliance

Clients come to psychotherapy or counseling in cases of infidelity with their stated or anticipated goal for treatment. This goal may or may not be a goal that is in their best interest or that is in line with the therapist's conceptualization of what is possible or aligned with the professional understandings of health and well-being. A misalignment of the goals between any of the parties bodes poorly for the therapeutic alliance, which is based on agreement of therapeutic goals and in-session tasks as well as the overall positive feelings of resonance between the client and therapist (Bordin, 1979; Horvath & Symonds, 1991; Horvath, 2005).

Some examples of these misalignments include the following pre-treatment stated goals that have occurred in my practice in the recent years for cases revolving around infidelity:

Stated Goal #1: A woman called to set up an appointment insisting that her husband come to therapy because she was certain he was having an affair. According to her he had little interest in participating in therapy. She wanted the therapist's help to convince him to come to therapy and to help him to face his responsibilities.

Two of the obvious issues in this early pre-treatment conversation are the lack of willingness on behalf of the husband (we surmise from her statement) and the inability ethically of the clinician to agree to the wife's stated objective because it is inconsistent with the clinical endeavor. The only possibility would be for the clinician to work with the wife individually to develop a working understanding of their issues, to build an alliance, and to suggest she invite her husband into therapy. While to a certain extent the willingness, or lack thereof, on the part of the husband may dictate the eventual unit of treatment (if he refuses to attend therapy, then no couples counseling can occur), the therapist has a role in this case in conceptualizing the wife's difficulties and in reframing the wife's stated goals as something more workable and clinically meaningful. In the early sessions establishing agreement on the "problem" and the treatment goals is paramount to a productive treatment alliance. If the wife is only willing to conceptualize the issues as his fault but he is unwilling to take part in the therapy, limited progress can be made on the relational issues. Progress, however, can be made on working through her feelings in this case and helping her to gain insight into what is possible in their relationship from an individual psychotherapeutic perspective.

Given that infidelity is often fraught with secrecy and denial before it is discovered, it is possible that the husband is having an affair and is hiding this from her. It may also be possible that she is entirely off base and is feeling insecure, obsessive, or even paranoid about this issue and no significant betrayal has occurred. With infidelity, the possibility always exists that clients harbor secrets and the therapist may never know enough of the details of what has occurred. In any case, there is a clear crisis and the therapist must remain open to what may be held secret even while empathizing with what is made transparent. Careful assessment, if possible, with both parties, both as a couple and in individual sessions, would be helpful in planning and considering additional factors. Factors that may be relevant to consider include relationship dynamics, historical patterns of infidelity, underlying psychopathology, personality structure, technology use, sexual satisfaction and behavior, and substance use, among others. Yet it is highly unlikely that adequate assessment and complete participation of both parties will be possible in a case like this one.

Another example of a client approaching therapy for infidelity concerns includes the following:

> Stated Goal #2: A man called to set up an appointment for him and his partner and wanted to use couples therapy to make sure that his partner never cheats again. He claims he is "over the affair" on the phone but he does not trust his partner and wishes to prevent anything like this from ever happening again. He is reluctant to attend to his own feelings or their relationship dynamics and instead continues to say that he wishes to use therapy to learn tools to monitor her behavior on an ongoing basis. He puts her on the phone and she is soft-spoken and introverted and unwilling to say much. She feels very ashamed of her behavior and is afraid of therapy.

The desire to assure that the other doesn't continue to have affairs and to monitor behavior is sometimes supported as a therapeutic intervention after a complete apology, and is designed to develop trust for the future (Glass, 2003). This particular set of interventions, however, creates a dynamic that is more akin to a parent and child dynamic and inherently supports a blaming and judgmental view of the partner who had the affair previously. While lying and cheating are not behaviors that therapy usually supports, monitoring behaviors between adults and reducing one to a subordinate subject is also problematic. With a stated goal such as this and ambivalence on the part of the partner, the clinician would likely have to work to provide space and support for the soft-spoken partner to share, while at the same time not alienating the partner who feels betrayed and rigid about his need for control. The therapist will have to work to support both to find their more vulnerable feelings and to work through them.

When one partner is quiet and the other controlling, as in this case, there is a need to assess for intimate partner violence (IPV). This would only be possible if the stated goal was shifted from monitoring behavior to facilitating authentic dialogue and healing early on. Because couples counseling is contraindicated in cases of IPV, and monitoring and controlling behavior could be a manifestation of IPV, it would be necessary to meet with each of the parties separately and to consider individual assessment. Because this approach is different than the stated goal and one partner is very afraid of therapy, the therapeutic alliance is immediately tenuous. If the therapist aligns with the stated goal, there are difficulties in the structural set-up of the therapy by implicitly further shaming and silencing one partner, supporting a potentially problematic power dynamic that is contraindicated by couples therapy, and fueling ongoing accusatory suffering (Stalfa & Hastings, 2005). The blame, apology, and monitor framework that is touted as helpful in some approaches to infidelity cases has the potential to be significantly problematic.

In the next example, an individual approaches therapy and does not wish to have his partner included. He has secrets to share and work through and does not want his partner to know about them at this juncture and maybe not ever.

> Stated Goal #3: A man came to individual therapy wanting to receive affirmation of his value and character despite the infidelity he was engaged in. This infidelity included lying and sneaking around behind his partner's back, which he himself judged negatively. At the same time he felt ambivalent about the idea of ending the affair, changing his circumstances, or working through feelings at any depth. He was deeply defensive and was reluctant to receive anything other than affirmation.

In this case the stated goal—to explore his behavior and judgment and come to a place of harmony relative to his promise of monogamy given the ambivalence—is realistic and appropriate for psychotherapy. The client's wish to have individual therapy rather than couples therapy given the secret he has, however, puts the therapist in an important position—a triangle relative to the partner and the client. Some clinicians suggest that insisting on ceasing the affairs or including the partner in such treatment plans is necessary for any progress to occur therapeutically (Glass, 2003). And yet others recognize that many clients have issues they wish to process in therapy before discussing with their partners and need some time to do so to make productive use of couples work if they choose to include their partner(s). Further, they may also not know what action they wish to achieve (e.g. divorce, break-up, reconciliation) and need to use the individual sessions to work that out before including the partner. Many clients are defensive and ambivalent about their behaviors, particularly infidelity, and sometimes this makes accessing feelings and developing insight difficult. At the same time, to provide support and affirmation only would be in effect sanctioning the affairs and therefore counter to the client's goals. The clinician would be positioned structurally like another outside party, triangulated in the relationship and making a warm receptive space that holds intimate secrets from the partner. This particular dynamic requires that the clinician balance the need for the client to explore and come to insight and the need to confront the dilemma. This will require making sure that the clinician continues to make the betrayed partner's perspective present in the sessions so that processing of difficult feelings can occur and the client can confront an occasion to integrate the potential impact he is having on his partner in his views. It also requires that the clinician consider options to address the dilemma with the client. The entire treatment can be framed not as a treatment for infidelity, then, but as a treatment for narcissistic features that make it challenging to impact the client or have him fully take in his potential impact on his partner and the fullness of the dilemma. Yet, if this is attempted too directly, or too soon, the defenses of this structure will make the alliance problematic, the client will leave therapy, or more defensiveness will occur. And yet the therapist is also obliged to not enable an affair to continue by acting as the third party supporting the structure through understanding. The physical or metaphoric inclusion of the perspective of the partner and the regular discussion of the need to confront the affair is important in these types of individual therapies. Eventually there may be an actual interest in suggesting couples work or the client may come to terms with the dilemma and may resolve it through structural means.

Another client reported Internet addiction in the call to set up an initial session and wanted help with treatment.

> Stated Goal #4: A man calls to say that he spends almost all of his time connected (e.g. online). He reports that he plays video games, watches a lot of porn, and spends a lot of time searching online late at night. Periodically during his searches he feels compelled to hire a dominatrix from Craigslist to humiliate and punish him. These sessions are not particularly sexual per se in that there is no penetration or touching really other than with a crop or paddle, but there is a sexual atmosphere and the sessions are thrilling and relieving. After these sessions he often can rest better, but then the tension builds over the next weeks again and he feels compelled to search and hire her again. He wants help with what he calls an "Internet addiction," worries that his girlfriend will leave him if she finds out, and that she will consider this to be a sexual betrayal even though it isn't sexual to him. His sex life with his girlfriend is very satisfying albeit not kinky.

Internet addiction is currently not a diagnostic category in the DSM-V (APA, 2013) and further there are many professionals who consider Internet addiction, video game addiction, porn addiction, sex addiction, and related phenomena to be misnomers and would rather all of these be categorized as problematic behaviors to be addressed best through Cognitive Behavioral Therapy (CBT) or harm reduction and mindfulness-based methods (Braun-Harvey & Vigorito, 2016) rather than through group therapy process-addiction models. Just because the client claims he has an Internet addiction does not mean this is necessarily the issue even if it is conceptualized alternatively as problematic Internet behavior, and even if in this case, he uses the Internet in an unconscious manner and spends many hours in front of the computer. In order to conceptualize treatment the clinician will have to consider how his technology use, need for humiliation, sexuality, and BDSM are related and which of these issues distress him, if any. It is possible that one or many of these behaviors and their sequelae are bothersome or related to other deeper developmental and relational issues and that the technology use is not the core issue. Sometimes the fear of judgment and the shame that prevents clients to articulate and meet a particular desire is the main issue.

It would be helpful to help him to map the antecedents and consequences of the thoughts, feelings, and sensations of the behavior coupled with harm reduction methods or mindfulness approaches for problematic technology use to begin assessment of such complex experiences. What exactly is problematic for him? What does he want to change? What are the consequences for him? What does he fear his girlfriend would think? Numerous studies support the idea that BDSM is a fetish but that risk-aware consensual BDSM is also not always problematic inherently or only insofar as the shame of being out about one's desires. It may be that the route to healing for this case is assessment of the source of discomfort of the compulsion to see a dominatrix. If it is solely from anticipated judgment of the girlfriend, then perhaps supporting his understanding of his proclivities, if they are not objectively problematic, leading to him telling his girlfriend about them, is important and would be integrative. Possibly this behavior could be understood as sexual and could also be understood as an aspect of his identity that he may need to explore. This particular case would require non-judgment from the perspective of the clinician. The girlfriend may or may not become part of a couples therapy (with another therapist) at some point.

These examples reflect some of the issues that may arise in early treatment planning as clients call or email to set up their first sessions. As noted earlier, often the first issue is to formulate a goal that is realistic and can be agreed upon and to define the unit of treatment. Sometimes this is problematic because some clinicians only work from a particular framework (e.g. EFT with couples) and cannot readily change and adapt to the circumstances that present themselves to offer psychodynamic therapy, CBT, or other methods and approaches to individuals, for example. In these cases, there is a need to collaborate with others and to make referrals as necessary.

To further complicate matters, sometimes people aren't sure what they want to accomplish because they don't know what therapy can provide in these upsetting circumstances or they cannot envision how things might develop and change through therapy. In all cases, clients have the same types of unexamined assumptions and biases as therapists (e.g. that monogamy is inherently problematic, that monogamy is the only right way to have a long-term relationship, that divorce is horrific, that people are inherently sexual or not, that cheaters are always cheaters, that affairs arise out of temptation, that sex is inherently less exciting over time in any relationship and can't be changed, and so on) and these inform what they expect.

In cases where the focus is on infidelity rather than other issues, more often than not competing interests exist in the treatment goals. For example, one party may want to receive a contrite apology and the other may have wanted to develop the sexual connection. The third party to the infidelity, while not usually involved in the treatment other than through second-hand discussions, often also has an impact, either directly or otherwise on the system. Careful consideration of these interests and how to support the system to attend to the many competing needs is important. Often it is best to hold hope for all possibilities and to suggest that those who call come to an initial session for assessment purposes and to neither commit to treating the client at this stage or not until a series of sessions can support a particular agreed-upon set of goals and a structure for treatment.

Assessment of Infidelity Cases

Assessment and treatment planning for infidelity cases is not entirely dissimilar to assessment of other types of psychological and relational phenomena. I will not diverge to deliver a course in psychological assessment at this point. However, there are a few considerations that are somewhat unique or important in cases of infidelity that merit mention.

1. Individual assessments: It is important to see couples together for at least one assessment session if possible and also to see each of the parties of the couple individually for at least one assessment session. I recommend making the number balanced and making the secrets policy and purpose of couples and individual sessions clear ahead of time. If you choose to not hold secrets between parties, this does not imply that a verbatim transcript of the individual sessions is provided to the other party, perhaps, but that the therapist uses these individual assessment sessions to help guide treatment planning decisions and may take up explicitly the issue of what and how to share the materials with one another for the greater good. Of critical import also is to help the individuals in each individual hour to metabolize issues and feelings they are having difficulty expressing or tolerating

in the couples sessions. If there is a great deal of difficulty with emotion regulation or if personality disorders are present in either or both parties, often referring out for individual work is a good next step.

2. Intimate partner violence: Make sure to assess for intimate partner violence and abuse. Sometimes sex, including affairs and other instances of infidelity as well as rape, sexual assault, and other forms of abuse, are used as tools of power in relationships. In these cases, treating the infidelity as infidelity is contraindicated. Conceptualize the issues instead as IPV or abuse and move forward accordingly. In these cases, couples therapy is also contraindicated.

3. History of infidelity: Consider the history of the relationship. How was the courtship, the quality of the original sexual connection? Has there been a history of ambivalence about commitment or jealousy of outsiders? How strong is their connection now? Have betrayals or triangulations featured prominently in the relationship or in other important relationships or families of origin? Many clinicians find that a sexual genogram or a sexual or relational history is important to collect so that the ongoing and intergenerational issues that may be relevant to infidelity become clear. Often infidelity can benefit from a systems or structural view.

4. Underlying psychopathology: Assess for any underlying psychopathology that might drive infidelity. There are a few symptom patterns that seem to correlate with experiences of infidelity. Consider ADHD and impulse control issues, bipolar disorder, substance use, and narcissistic personality disorder, among other possibilities for the one who had the affair. Consider depression, OCD, substance use, and Autism Spectrum Disorder, among other possibilities, for the one who was betrayed. These are not exhaustive but they can result in affairs among other problematic relational experiences if untreated. If there are additional diagnoses, consider treating these as well if they fit within your scope of competency or consider referring out to address them. Infidelity that occurs within a manic episode should be conceptualized and treated differently than infidelity that occurs from within an existential crisis or a substance binge.

5. Recent stressors: Capture any recent stressors that preceded the affair(s) such as deaths, grief reactions, job losses, health concerns, trauma, war, births, and other existentially fraught events, in particular. Sex, power, birth, and death seem to be somewhat related and many philosophers have noted that there are connections between powerful meaningful events, and oftentimes affairs relate to existential crises. Sometimes people have affairs because they feel afraid of death and the foreclosing of possibilities that is palpable at particular developmental junctures. Sometimes people assert sexual vitality and choices as a metaphoric reaction to death.

6. The role of technology in sex and relationships: Ask how the Internet and other technologies impact the lives and relationships of the client(s). Consider how technology was used in the affair, in particular. While we all collectively have a number of technology habits that may be questionable, or problematic, and we have very little information about the long-term effects of our behaviors psychologically, some clients are strikingly out of control with their behaviors. If needed, refer to a qualified clinician who has expertise in assessing and treating problematic technology behavior. Be wary, however, of assigning the label "addict." There is simply not enough evidence that sex addiction or Internet addiction are the most fitting frameworks for these phenomena. Often a basic assessment of the antecedents and consequences of various aspects of technology use is helpful in determining if there is distress or issues related to technology use as a separate or related issue to infidelity. CBT interventions as well as harm reduction interventions are often helpful in cases where there are technology issues.

7. Sex: Ask about sexual satisfaction and desires directly. What is the idealized version of how sex should be as compared to how sex actually is or was with the primary partner at the time of the affair? Try to understand if sex is central to the problem or tangential and if the sexual difficulties are self-similar to any other difficulties in the relationship or restricted only to the sexual realm. And in what ways is sex problematic in the relationship now? If needed, refer to a qualified sex therapist who has expertise in assessing and treating sexual issues, particularly if couples therapy is not progressing as expected or there are problems with sexual functioning (e.g. arousal, desire, orgasm).

8. What is hidden: Consider the role of secrecy and social desirability in your planning. It is likely that within the first few assessment sessions your client offers a limited view of the actual internal experience of having had an affair. Yet it is upon these initial sessions that we make our treatment plan and select the unit of treatment. It is entirely possible that more and different material will be uncovered through the therapy process in an ongoing manner. There may be a need to provide individual therapy to support a more authentic discussion of the experience without the social desirability pressures inherently present in couples work.

9. Consider strengths and goals: Determine if the couple or client is volatile and has the ego strength and insight into what occurred as well as the requisite emotion regulation skills to process the details before attempting anything like a full disclosure or apology. Also consider if a full disclosure is really necessary. Is building trust possible without full disclosure—or even perhaps in some ways better—because

then the one who was betrayed isn't plagued by the details of the experience that he or she will likely obsessively replay later throughout the relationship? The risk of ongoing seeking of details of the affair, being haunted by those details, seeking more apology, and cycling into more and more hurt and upset is very real. Some couples can handle a full disclosure and can give and receive an apology. Some have far too much trauma and underlying attachment issues to go directly for this goal at the outset. Consider if, how, and when to approach these frequently desired experiences in the context of capacity to handle them.

10. Facilitate dialogue: If possible, begin to facilitate a dialogue that is productive, that builds intimacy and connection, and that helps metabolize the vulnerable feelings and confusion. EFT, Gottman method, Imago, or other means may be relevant. EFT is the most frequently cited in the literature for success in treating infidelity in couples from among these. Any of these can be used in conjunction with the directions from the phenomenological findings.

11. Consider early relationships: Consider also the idea of psychodynamic or psychoanalytic work if there appears to be an interest and need for deeper understandings. Many of the roots of infidelity can be found in early relational experiences. For some this is an important step.

All of these structural and assessment considerations are important before considering the application of the findings from my phenomenological research. Once you have assessed and conceptualized the treatment accordingly, you have room to consider the underlying issues that give rise to the experience of infidelity in the first place.

Using Phenomenological Research to Direct Treatment of Infidelity

The findings from the previous chapter suggest that there is a nuanced and complex process that occurs for the one who betrays his or her partner that makes possible the justification for and gives rise to the affair. This process is set in motion through a series of perceptions that precede and co-occur with the affair. The affair is in effect potentiated by the existence of these perceptions. This implies that while people enter therapy often wanting to address the behavior and feelings that result from the infidelity, beneath this lie a set of *problematic perceptions* that support one another structurally and give rise to the conditions that made the affair possible. These perceptions warrant attention if there is to be any transformation—this is the essence of the new treatment direction.

The idea is that to simply address the regret, hurt, or problematic behaviors may still leave the problematic *perceptions* for the person who had the affair unvoiced, secret from the partner, and fundamentally intact in an ongoing manner. For this reason, shifting the perceptions of the one who engaged in infidelity is the goal in the new treatment direction. The focus on perceptions potentiating the affairs is not the same as stating that people are not responsible for their actions because they were misperceiving. Of course those who have affairs are ultimately responsible for their behaviors regardless of which perceptions they hold. The ability to think, plan, act, and empathically consider our impact on others is what separates us as humans. However, we are also not always conscious of how our various perceptions tend to add up to constitute a particular set of perceived options and choices, which then lead to behaviors and choices we sometimes regret. We are not always adept at accurately perceiving risk.[1] In essence, it is possible that the context of how affairs develop is a result of our difficulties with perceiving risk in advance accurately.

Recall the perceptions that co-occur with infidelity for the one who begins an affair.

1. Dissatisfaction and hopelessness in the relationship.
2. A value of novelty and passion in romantic/sexual relationships.
3. A sense of deserving sexual satisfaction or intimate connection.
4. The partner and self are viewed as fixed characters.
5. Lack of curiosity for the partner as a person with their own subjectivity.
6. An experience of desire and passion overriding and overtaking one's judgment.
7. The affair is not recognized as an affair until after it begins.
8. Divorce or opening up the primary relationship are not considered options for structural resolution of the issues.

What is wonderful about these perceptions (or any, for that matter) is that they can change or can be prompted to change with sufficient exploration, reflection, and challenge. This is one of the agenda items for psychotherapeutic work with clients who have experienced infidelity implied by this research. If Giorgi (2009) is correct in his articulation of the phenomenological research method discussed in chapter 4, by stating that all of the essential constituents from a phenomenological analysis are required to define the phenomenon and that they support one another structurally to constitute and maintain the phenomenon, then it is also true that to shift any of the constituents of the experience weakens the structure and gives rise to a different structure or phenomenon at an essential level.

It is shifting these perceptions that I wish to place in the center of new directions for treatment and specifically in opposition to forced apology and forgiveness until the constituents of infidelity have shifted. I also want to help people to become more conscious of the choice points they engage on the small and larger levels within their relationships along the way, and to become more adept at predicting and anticipating how they might feel in advance so that they can navigate experiences with more insight in the future. This approach is in contrast to behavioral monitoring of the one who engaged in infidelity that sometimes is used.

Beneath this entire approach is the deep belief that "faulty" or problematic perceptions and behaviors are the person's best attempt to navigate their own internal prohibitions, psychological material, and contextual stressors. Shifting perceptions that potentiate an affair requires that the therapist hold hope that there is a way out of the dilemma suggested by the constituents (or perhaps many ways) and that the direction out of the dilemma will be through shifting perceptions of the dilemma. In particular the hope that therapists are to hold is not only that there are many ways out of the dilemma through shifts in the eight constituents, but also that some of these ways may include solutions that would not be personally comforting to the therapist but may suit the client's needs very well (e.g. opening up the relationship, reconciling, or divorce).

What follows is each of the constituents taken one at a time, followed by considerations of assessment and treatment planning with respect to the goal of shifting the perception in question and encountering the barriers that allowed the perception to manifest. The assumption is that this particular person has not only kept the affair secret but more importantly has not been able to make fully transparent the set of feelings and perceptions that potentiated the affair. Making these conscious and shared allows the couple to engage a more complete understanding of their issues. While these particular perceptions are thought to be structurally essential to the development of infidelity, I surmise that one or another of them may not resonate strongly with a particular client. Determining which of the eight constituents are most resonant for any particular client will guide treatment priorities, after the initial assessments.

Dissatisfaction and Hopelessness in the Relationship

Therapists are often coached to hold hope for couples who have experienced infidelity to reconcile (Glass, 2003)—which is implied as hope that they have an infidelity-free future. Clients often come to marriage or couples counseling with the implicit idea that their relationships will be supported and that monogamy will be emphasized, and this is certainly intuitive and often desired. However, this particular hope skips over the feelings of the person who engaged in infidelity. Their dissatisfaction and hopelessness about the primary relationship do not vanish because their affair is discovered, even though they may feel and say that they wish to reconcile and return to the previous arrangement. The concerns about whether or not the couple can heal after an affair or whether or not they can avoid infidelity in the future are usually more aligned with the per-spective and needs of the one who has been betrayed. The dissatisfaction and hopelessness about the primary relationship felt by the one who has had the affair, as noted in the research findings, began before the affair and ostensibly are still present. This dissatisfaction includes the idea that there is hopelessness about ever having a novel, vital, and passionate sexual connection within the primary relationship. Further, the one who begins an affair believes that the partner is less capable or less willing to engage these parts of the relationship. If the therapist fails to facilitate exploration of the feelings of unmet sexual and erotic desires at some point in the therapy, and also fails to explore the shadow side of the pos-sibilities within this worry, then the particular dissatisfaction and hope-less feelings will most likely remain somewhat in secret underground, for the one who began the affair, even if there is hope that the couple can heal or that they can get through the hurt feelings brought about by the discovery of infidelity.

Because clinicians are not trained to address sexual concerns, most will lack the skills to assess and treat issues of desire, eroticism, and sexuality and will cast this kind of issue as an attachment issue, a medical issue, or an issue with the underlying connection between the partners. They will likely dutifully approach the problem by trying to build connection and intimacy through helping clients to become vulnerable and to attend to each other's feelings and needs. Or they will work psychodynamically on early relationships. None of this is the wrong direction. Likely most couples could benefit from building a stronger connection and sense of attunement and development of the capacity to access their vulnerabilities and process their feelings of early upsets. Yet developing and facilitating eroticism, managing desire discrepancies, and facilitating fulfilling sexual engage-ments may require a set of different interventions and considerations—and sometimes these are simply what is needed to move the perception of hopelessness to hopefulness. In short, clinicians may need to refer to a sex therapist or to learn more about sexuality themselves.

Establishing hope for change in this particular perception can be explicitly stated (without overpromising results and stepping into unethi-cal territory) and requires that clinicians actually believe that it is pos-sible, even if only theoretically in the beginning. This requires bracketing any beliefs or ideas we have about the meaning of stagnant sexual rela-tionships, inherent chemistry, and beliefs about the meaning of affairs and monogamy. Hope is also communicated implicitly by the questions asked and the focus of the clinical work and by the range of ideas that get explored. If the partner who had the affair is supported in expressing his or her or their concerns—and the focus is not only on repair of the trust and creating safety and prevention of subsequent affairs but also on building eroticism and adventure—then there is room to reconsider the original hopelessness that we surmise made the affair possible in the first place. This begets hope for the possibility of a vital sexual connection and may drive other changes in the perceptions held by the one who engaged in infidelity.

In addition to clinicians receiving little training in addressing sexual issues, collectively as a culture we have a great number of judgments and fears about sexual function and desire. We tend to idealize desire in movies and porn, and many of our sexual encounters in real life do not live up to these examples. We are not perfectly in tune with our partners (most of us anyway) and sometimes experience desire discrepancies and disappointments. Many people have very little clue what they desire, how to talk about desires if they are aware of them, how to drive desire when it feels elusive, or what to do with ongoing unmet desires, and yet these kinds of issues are problematic for long-term sexually monogamous relationships if they go unaddressed. What makes these issues even more troubling is that many people believe a host of incorrect ideas about sexual behavior and sexual desire that make exploration of these issues difficult. They include a series of fixed ideas that are not accurate or could be contested according to contemporary research of sexual function and behavior. Commonly held beliefs about sexuality I have heard in my practice include:

- People inherently have more or less sexual desire and this does not change.
- Sexual desire always wanes in long-term relationships.
- Men normally have more sexual desire than women.
- Men who have less desire than women are sissies, less virile, or have a porn problem.
- Women who enjoy sex are bad, slutty, dirty, or will tempt others' husbands and partners into infidelities. They also were not parented correctly and represent loose morals or were sexually abused.
- Gay men are always interested in sex.
- Lesbians have very little sex and can expect lesbian bed death to occur in long-term relationships.
- Some people are inherently good lovers and others are not, and this cannot or does not change.
- You have to be good-looking or in shape to have good sex or to be desirable.
- Penis size matters.
- Breast size matters.
- Members of different ethnic groups have sex differently, have a different appetite for sex, and are therefore more or less desirable to others.

The list continues. None of these statements are true, even though certain people may agree with each of them and there are individual cases of life experience that support each; however, there are just as many cases that support alternative views and we are not always privy to cases outside of our own experience. What is significantly problematic about these views is that they are based on stereotypes, focus on the physical aspects of sexuality as portrayed in media and porn, and largely ignore the most important aspect of sexuality and desire that can change and is within our control, which occurs in the mind through fantasy and creativity. In addition, these faulty beliefs ignore the contextual variables that are related to desire. The arguments are largely deterministic and therefore do not offer much opportunity for development or change. It is easy to feel hopeless if these are the beliefs that underpin how we view sex.

Sexologists have a longstanding debate about the relative impact of biological forces as compared to social forces on our experiences of sexual desire, sexual behavior, and sexual satisfaction.[2] Most researchers, sex educators, and sex therapists agree that people can learn sexual skills, to develop and articulate desires, and that desire and satisfaction can wax and wane over time. Sometimes helping people to uncover unrealistic beliefs about sex, learn new skills, and try new approaches redefines their experiences entirely. To the CBT-oriented therapist this is not a monumental idea. However, not all CBT practitioners have sufficient understanding of their own faulty beliefs about sexuality to recognize appropriate interventions in areas of sexuality.

Some interventions designed to shift these perceptions to impact the sense of hopelessness might include:

• What came before the affair?: Meet with the one who began the affair and ask him or her or them to discuss the feelings about the primary relationship that preceded the affair without the other present. This allows the therapist to uncover what underlies the affair, which of the phenomenological findings is most relevant to begin with, and can help facilitate their discussion in couples therapy later. It is important to ask if they have discussed any dissatisfaction and hopelessness issues as a couple before, how that discussion went, and what the perceived barriers were to making changes to accommodate the yearnings of both. Usually clients report one or two discussions, and that the other party responded with something that shut the dialogue down, and it then began to feel impossible to make progress. Many couples are afraid of conflict and simply prefer to give up on the dialogue. Facilitating the dialogue can be helpful.
• Consider dissatisfaction: Assess directly the specific dissatisfactions that the one who had the affair experiences. Often people are unable

to voice these concerns concretely, even in an individual format, for many reasons: They lack language to describe their desires; they find their desires unacceptable and fear judgment; or they feel their desires are unreasonable, but they nevertheless have them so they half-step in their articulation of them. The same forces that made this issue difficult to discuss and hopeless to solve (as perceived by the one who has the affair) are still at play and may make the discussion in therapeutic contexts also challenging. People tend to use vague language to refer to sexuality concerns and worry about judgment and shame with the therapist. Often they will initially report: "We were just disconnected and I felt alone," or "It didn't feel close or intimate anymore and I didn't know how to change that." Most therapists make the mistake of not asking more about how the disconnect presents itself or what the person wishes for in terms of connection. In consultation groups and discussions with colleagues it is apparent that therapists often assume "a connection" implies talking and feeling close and safe when it could also mean connection through an experience of passion and adventure, or sexual and physical connection, or even connection through conflict and authenticity. Therapists might instead follow up with additional exploratory questions such as: "How much of the issue did you experience as a disconnect in a sexual or erotic sense, and how much of the issue would you say was a more general disconnect in terms of lack of time spent together or inability to share thoughts and experiences?" One might also ask, "What would your fantasy have been before the infidelity about connecting with your partner?" And even, "What barriers did you perceive existed to having that fantasy become reality?" These questions will help you get a sense of what was desired. Often these questions evoke interesting and helpful dialogue that has not been discussed by the couple. Usually people have not been particularly precise with their partners about their desires and also have not been able to persevere through a productive conversation about the barriers on both sides to having sexuality and eroticism work for both parties.

- Articulate desires concretely: Address desires directly and help clients to unpack them more concretely. Sometimes the desires are experienced as somewhat concrete and the work is to consider them and the barriers to their fulfillment (e.g. "I just want to know that you are willing to be flexible sometimes and that sex doesn't always have to be exactly the same."). In this case, what constitutes variety and how the couple comes to decide and communicate what will occur sexually, and the flexibility of the script, is a potentially fruitful area to explore. Other times the desires are felt as concrete desires and can be addressed as such, but also could be a stand-in or metaphor for something deeper. For example, wanting the partner to take control during sex could be a concrete desire that could be considered and negotiated or might relate to another issue of feeling that all the responsibilities at work are burdensome and the partner wants someone else to be in charge, and this becomes the area of intervention instead. Having a fantasy about being younger and fitter could be related to concerns about aging and death, which informs the areas of exploration. Asking if these desires need to be fulfilled concretely often helps. Considering the psychodynamic realms relating to the fantasies is also helpful in guiding the therapist to discern the difference between actual needs and metaphors. Sometimes the desires are simply unreasonable or problematic (e.g. "I just want to have sex whenever I want, how I want, and I don't want to have to deal with his needs!") and suggest that there is a particular problematic dynamic in the relationship or underlying issue that warrants attention. Often in these sessions it becomes clear that the desires are felt in a particular manner (e.g. fantasies of younger men), but may need to be worked with to see if they themselves shift to make room for a different set of perceptions. What was once hopeless to achieve can then be possible if the desire itself is understood and metabolized psychologically and transforms to another desire or can be articulated and addressed directly. Sometimes this shift results in the couple realizing that they are in fact incompatible (e.g. one wants to have a particular kind of sex and the other doesn't, and they don't have the stamina to consider this more deeply so they simply want to part ways). Other times it opens up a vital novel connection because newness is available again.

An example from my practice follows:

A couple that had been married for approximately a decade (each second marriages) had reached a crisis. The wife threatened to move out, and there was a fair amount of hostility and anger on her part and confusion on his. They came to couples counseling as a last ditch effort to see if they could make some changes, and at the very least to be sure that the move toward separation was indeed the right decision. I spent a few sessions dedicated to assessment and evaluation of their dynamic and collecting the concerns that had accumulated over the years, and helped to soften their communication dynamic through principles of EFT and non-violent communication. I also spent time helping them to develop emotion regulation techniques so that they could stay productive in their conversations. During these initial sessions, they made some progress but not enough to decide one way or another about staying married or divorcing. She felt abandoned by him when he made decisions without her and when he retreated to watch TV, go online, or work late, which he did often. She suspected he was having an affair and he denied this. He felt maligned and afraid of her temper, since she would explode periodically with a list of unmet needs and stored complaints that were baffling to him.

I met with each of them individually for one session to listen to what might be unsaid in the couples format and to deepen my understanding of their perspectives. During these sessions we discussed their disappointments without the other present to react, thus interrupting their reactive dynamic. It was easier to gather and explore the issues in a more vulnerable manner in this format.

She was hurt that he didn't consider her and didn't make time for her. She felt he was selfish and inconsiderate, and this fueled her anger and sense of injustice. It also activated early trauma of neglect and a damaged sense of her self-worth. She wanted my help to make progress in compelling him to take her viewpoint, and she wanted to be sure he was not cheating. In addition, she noted that she was not ready to leave imminently but that she felt only half committed to staying. I asked her about their early courtship and about their sexual connection, which was solid in the beginning. She noted that he ate a ton of junk food and was now pre-diabetic, overweight, and had erectile dysfunction (ED). She saw this as another way he was selfish and demonstrated his lack of care for her. If he really loved her, she reasoned, he would take care of himself so that he could perform. She wanted to have a sexual relationship with him and to feel desired and found the ED to be the greatest disappointment of all.

It surprised me that she didn't voice her feelings about sex upfront in our couples session. Perhaps because they were so hostile and slept in separate rooms at this point, it was easier to tend to the issues they raised that particular day rather than ask about sex; it took me asking directly about sex after a few sessions to get this topic into the room. I asked if she had told him about her desires to have a sexual relationship with him and she replied no. She felt so upset, yet it was not clear to him that she still wanted him sexually. She noted that she didn't want to approach him with her desires and have him go soft and then feel the old feelings of abandonment and lack of worth through his lack of arousal. She also knew that it was humiliating for him to not be able to perform. Her silence on the issue was a way to protect him from shame.

In my individual session with him, I asked him about his concerns. He felt that he could not satisfy her with her many requests and complaints, which he experienced as out of the blue and confusing. He is a very highly gifted scientist and often has his head in the clouds—some of the nuances of pragmatic language and social interactions seemed to escape him, so it was easy to see how these complaints would be confusing from his perspective. While he was a kind, warm, and jovial man, he felt very hurt that his attempts at connection were largely met with complaints and hostility. I asked him about their early courtship and their sexual connection. For him, this was a wonderful time period. He noted that sex was always a strength for them until recently. He divulged that he had ED and didn't want to go through the shame of attempting to engage sexually with her and then fail to achieve an erection. He avoided any discussion of this with her and said that she seemed to avoid it too. He figured that he had one or two instances of ED a few years ago, and that marked the beginning of the end of sexuality for them; he reasoned that this was related to aging and that it was inevitable. He spent a great deal of time fantasizing about their earlier days when she was thinner and had fewer complaints, and when they had a passionate, engaging, and frequent sexual connection. He felt guilty that he was so critical of her appearance when he himself is older and heavier, and he didn't dare to voice these concerns with her directly. I wondered aloud with him if he would find her attractive if she were the same physically but was kinder and more passionate with him. I also suggested that the mind is a great tool for facilitating desire. He agreed that those were the more important variables and that he was aware that they were both far more good-looking ten years ago and that he still finds her appealing. I designed this particular discussion to assure that his fantasies were somewhat realistic and balanced lest he activate what for many is a cycle of body dysmorphia that comes on full force with aging that is often applied to women more than men. I asked him if he ever had erections (e.g. in the morning, in response to fantasies) to which he noted that he did. I also asked if he masturbated to which he replied that he did. I asked if he watched porn and he noted that he rarely did, but from time to time he would. He often played online solitaire, however, to clear his mind and had several fantasy sports teams. He noted that because his wife was so worried that he was having an affair, he would often hide all of his online activities from her, which he suspected fueled her suspicions further. I also asked if he'd had his blood pressure checked recently and he reported he had.[3]

When they came together in the next session, I asked them to share a synopsis of what we had discussed and suggested that an interesting dynamic was occurring. Sexually, they were experiencing a self-similar dynamic to what occurred in the arguments—she felt neglected and unwanted, and he felt like he was not enough to satisfy her and feared failing her. And they had a mistaken belief about what was possible for them sexually. She believed he would never get erect because he had a few instances of ED and that he didn't care enough for her inherently. He thought her lack of approaching him meant that she was unwilling to tolerate his intermittent ED. Once they realized that they *could* have intercourse, and that many people experience intermittent ED that comes and goes, they brightened up. I sent them home to do homework to explore and imagine individually what it would be like to engage with one another sexually again. I imagined that they would come up with fears and desires that we would process over several sessions working toward changing the dynamic to see how working with the sexuality would impact the rest of their issues. I was also still holding the possibility that he was having an affair (online, porn, or in the flesh) because of how reserved he is about his schedule and how he retreats from her, but so far did not hear anything to support this idea except her suggestions. I anticipated that any win in the physical realm would translate into a win in their conversations.

They returned the following week and sat very close to one another on the couch for the first time ever, grinning and reporting that the homework seemed silly to them so they just skipped it and had sex for the first time in many years. While they felt some fear about whether he would stay hard, and he did experience a short moment of difficulty, they felt motivated and able to stay present in the sexual connection through the doubts and the ebb and flow of the erection. While they felt rusty in some ways, this new connection made it possible for them to be motivated to engage the other dynamics. We were then able to make progress on the list of other issues much more quickly. They had embodied sexually the same healing dynamic that needed to occur in conversation—they needed to stay in the difficult parts and trust that both wanted to work through it. In this case, working with sexuality directly facilitated movement more quickly in the conversations. It also had the effect of him spending less time retreating to the computer privately, which for both of them was a source of shame and concern. In the end, she let go of the fear that he was having an affair because they felt more connected and they were able to make progress on the other concerns they had stored up over the years.

Working directly with sexuality and in particular with the original disappointment makes possible the authentic voice of the one who had the affair, or who is perceived to be engaging in infidelity, to come forward. This is perhaps not something that usually occurs in couples therapy in part because of the goals of couples therapy are often antithetical to the goals of developing eroticism to a certain extent. It is surprising how quickly people give up trying and come to believe that their partner is a fixed unchangeable entity rather than that perhaps there is something problematic about their conversation or some other barriers that are beneath the discussion that if shifted may give rise to other possibilities. Often helping one party to voice the desire for eroticism in a productive manner and to facilitate a dialogue about the barriers is at the root of the infidelity. And sometimes there is sexual trauma, sexual skill deficits, fear of intimacy, or difficulties with eroticism that require concrete attention and support. Helping the one who had the affair to see the situation as not fixed and that before sexual foreplay is a series of activities that make eroticism possible is critical. The clinician can help couples to backward map through the barriers what is needed to get into a state that makes an erotic atmosphere possible. Oftentimes people lack self-care or don't feel playful; have not flirted in a long time; feel burdened by the act of beginning a sexual act; are constricted by sexual scripts; and yearn for freedom, novelty, and transcendence. The therapist can help translate and interpret these barriers and/or give targeted skills or homework to address them depending on their theoretical orientation.

It also is a gift to complain well—although many don't receive it that way. It is the first thread of risking reaching out and trying for change and being seen in one's experience in a vulnerable way, and it precedes the more problematic state—hopelessness and giving up. When we get curious about another's complaint and treat it as information about their internal state, which we do not have to satisfy outright but might engage, we can collaborate and potentially find our way back to connection. Without this intimate offering, we cannot engage authentically because we don't actually know the other in this moment. It is this skill that needs honing and shaping therapeutically and which may require some direction, interrupting, slowing down, emotion regulation, and guidance so that the conversation can be productive.

Within all the cases of infidelity often there is a lack of sharing of concerns in a deep and meaningful and tenacious manner. People report getting up the guts to say one time perhaps to their spouse that they want to have more sex, or a few times that they feel lonely and want passion, and when this isn't addressed by their spouse changing something, they give up because it is too vulnerable to keep asking or they have no idea how to go about impacting the experience. What they don't understand is that it is one of the most common issues to have desire discrepancies in relationships, and often one or two conversations are insufficient to address them. Being tenacious about encouraging the couple to deepen their dialogue about the issues and to investigate the layers of related issues is also a form of intimacy, and the ongoing discussion about the issues and the barriers to their movement often keeps the hopelessness at bay because a new kind of conversation occurs.

A Value of Novelty and Passion in Romantic/Sexual Relationships

Perel (2007) and Morin (1996), among others, suggest that there are opposing forces in long-term sexual relationships—closeness, attunement, and safety on one side, and on the other side of the dynamic there is surprise, passion, and adventure. In cases of infidelity, often the latter side of the dynamic is not present in the primary relationship but gets activated in the experience of infidelity. This part of experience requires that we have sufficient distance to objectify the partner somewhat in order to fantasize or to animate a protentional set of vital possibilities for the future. This is experienced as eroticism or desire. This process begins for us when we see the other in a particular light (usually not literally) as a desirable other, a sexual object, a playful partner full of potential, and therefore can animate options that may arise, and with whom we can dynamically engage in an adventure. It is the stuff of witty banter, flirting, suggestive gesture, and play.

Closeness and safety, for example, is thought to be somewhat antithetical to this force of eroticism in that safety is predicated on predictability, and eroticism is to a certain extent predicated on novelty. Of course, objectifying the partner too much without safety and connection is also problematic. Neither polarity is sufficient without the other. When this particular dynamic is too collapsed and enmeshed, whether positive or negative (e.g. lovey-dovey or critical and controlling), there is no room to see the other as a desirable other because he or she is an extension of ourselves and not distant enough to provide the space to see the other as separate (to objectify) or as a somewhat unknown creative other. Too much distance in relationships does not provide enough connection at all (erotic or otherwise). Facilitating development of eroticism for couples and sensitivity to these two aspects of relationships requires attention to the side of the dynamic that psychotherapists are less familiar with.

This particular constituent includes the perception from the point of view of the one who engaged in infidelity that novelty and passion is important and further that he or she or they are inherently more passionate, interesting, and interested in the world than the other. Usually this particular view arises out of a dynamic that includes the couple occupying different points on the introversion/extroversion scale or taking different positions on the value of responsibility versus fun. When this becomes viewed as synonymous with each person's personality or inflexible, it becomes a problem. While it may be true that some people are more extroverted, less anxious, and more apt to play, relational dynamics can shift to make space for more introverted persons to come forward, for creating the context for playfulness and adventure, and for shifting the responsibilities and collective anxieties around them.

Some interventions for this particular constituent might include:

- Fore-foreplay: Ask a couple to consider what they need in order to be ready to engage in playfulness and an erotic mindset. For some, this requires getting to a place of what I call fore-foreplay. The idea is that whomever in the dynamic seems to have the greater sense of responsibility for the mundane duties of life and whomever in the dynamic seems to hold the greater sense of anxiety will be potentially less free to engage erotically and passionately. Anxiety can be co-regulated in a relationship and sometimes addressing a rebalancing of anxiety and responsibilities can have an enormous effect on couples. Often the one who is more playful and easygoing is not apt to want to take up the anxiety or responsibilities easily, however, so sometimes outsourcing tasks or connecting them to a shared understanding of sex and passion being possible and linked is important.
- Early dating stories: Help couples to explore their early experiences with each other, particularly if they were passionate and exciting (and often they are in the beginning) and to understand the contextual and situational variables of that experience so that they can recreate these types of situations. This is why inspired dates or making an effort to flirt with one another can sometimes rejuvenate a relationship.
- Fantasy: Develop a sense of fantasy. Sometimes people have specific fantasies and other times they have difficulty accessing fantasies, allowing themselves to fantasize, or articulating fantasies. Working with fantasies both as metaphors and as actual scenes they may wish to actualize can facilitate development of hope and help each partner to come alive. Developing the willingness and practice to cultivate fantasies and eroticism is key for couples who wish to develop after an affair regardless of whether they remain together or not, and this work can be facilitated by the therapeutic endeavor.
- Explore what is denied or prohibited: Sometimes underlying problems with passion include the fear of unchecked desires or the social prohibitions of sexual desires. There has been a strong mistrust through religious and social learning of any impulses that reside in the body, and these messages make it challenging for some to allow for passion and play in their relationships. Exploring these barriers and prohibitions directly can sometimes be helpful.
- Sexual trauma: The pervasively experienced sexual assault and rape of women and sometimes men can cause difficulties for people to embrace desire and passion and playfulness in an erotic sense without activating fears and traumas. Assessment and working through these kinds of traumas can be helpful for some and sometimes underlie the experiences of infidelity.

Here is another example of how hopelessness can be voiced and worked on individually and then discussed with the couple:

Therapist: As you know, J and I met last week, just like you and I met the week before. We discussed some of his feelings about your connection before the affair. I want to spend today seeing if we can have a conversation that helps us develop the connection and to shift some of the stuckness about the issue. Would that be OK? OK. Turn to your partner, J, and see if you can give voice to the feelings we discussed when we met last time.

J: OK. So, essentially, I had the feeling that I just kept trying to engage you and you kept pushing me away. I felt unwanted and silly trying over and over so I just gave up after a while. I really felt like I was unattractive and lecherous with my desires because you seemed so disgusted. It was a horrible feeling. So I went online a lot because I could feel attractive interacting with those women.

P: OK. (To the therapist—agitated) But what do you want me to say? I am not going to have sex just to make him feel better! That doesn't feel right. And I don't want him chatting with random women just because I didn't give him what he needs!

Therapist: Let's slow down a bit. It looks like his sharing his feelings evoked something in you. Can we pause for a minute? What is coming up right now?

P: I feel pressure—boxed in. And angry. It's like his needs take precedence over mine.

Therapist: OK. Pressured. Like his needs take precedence. So I want to go really slowly now. Can we just check to make sure that you received what he said as he intended it? We will come back to what was evoked. I think it's very important. Is that OK?

P: Sure. So, I heard you say that you felt awful and pushed away and that you gave up eventually approaching me for sex? Is that right?

J: Mostly, but it's actually more than just sex. It's like I wanted to play and have fun and you are always so serious and responsible. I felt like you were rejecting all the good parts and only wanted me for the responsibilities and tasks you need. Like a work horse.

P: OK. I want that too but I can't get to that if there is so much work to do with the kids and the house and so on.

Therapist: OK. So, stay there in the dilemma. I see that his desire to have fun with you evokes a barrier for you—the work, the

kids, and all that remains not attended to, that for you precedes sex and fun. Is that right?

P: Yes.

Therapist: I am hearing something slightly different though. It seems
                like you both want sex and fun but that you have a different
                order of operations sometimes. Is that the case?

P: (nodding)

J: (nodding)

Therapist: And say a bit more about the first barrier that came up. The
                one about needing to have sex because he wants it.

P: Sure. It's kind of like I don't want to have to have respon-
                sibility for his sexual satisfaction. I want to have sex when
                I want it and to not have to have it just because he wants
                it. Since I never have all the tasks done I almost never feel
                relaxed enough to want it. It feels like a burden.

J: (Throws his hands up in the air and rolls his eyes) But it will
                never all be done!

Therapist: OK. So that brought up something for you, J. Let's slow
                down and get curious. It sounds like you are afraid that she
                won't desire you ever and yet I heard her say that she wants
                to want it but needs some relief from the responsibilities to
                get there. Oddly enough it sounds like you are both wanting
                to be free from some responsibilities. Is that right?

J: (deep sigh and relaxing)

P: I think that would be amazing!

In this example, the couple discusses the tension between responsibilities and play that so many overworked and stressed couples face.
This particular dynamic is important to understand because the issue is
upstream from foreplay in the ability for each of them to get into a shared
understanding of what it takes to be ready to engage and to facilitate
that with each other. For J there may be readiness to engage without as
much concern about responsibilities and an ability to let go. For P, there
is some concern that she may not be taken care of or supported in their
collective responsibilities and she also has a responsibility to be a sexual
partner. Helping her to articulate what she needs to be available sexually
is important, and helping them both to understand that they both want
to connect sexually will help the hopelessness fade.

The therapist needs to be very active in the session, directing the conversation at key difficult moments of sharing so that authentic feelings
can be shared and reactions can be managed. Without a facilitator, either
of the parties might become very activated, and the conversation could
become very polar, further cementing the hopelessness. Helping clients to
slow down, get curious about their feelings, listen to one another, ask for

clarification, and deepen into vulnerable discussions is paramount and may require some direction from therapists.

A Sense of Deserving Sexual Satisfaction or Intimate Connection

The interesting part of this particular perception is the felt sense of deserving. While monogamy combined with desires that are unmet and no other perceived channel to meet them within the relationship can cause significant frustration, deserving implies something more. At the same time, it also diminishes the subjectivity of the partner who, from this perspective, is unwilling or unable to satisfy. When we promise monogamy, we are not guaranteed happiness or satisfaction, even if it is the implicit goal or desired state. Regardless of the circumstances, there are a great number of ways we can impact our expectations and experience of sexual satisfaction, as well as ways in which we cannot control our partner or many of the circumstantial variables that may impact our experiences. For example, if we are injured and sexual behavior becomes uncomfortable or limited, then perhaps the route to sexual satisfaction may include both acceptance of some limitations and adjustment of expectations and creative adaptation. Throughout life there are many of these types of circumstances. While it is important that we all strive toward satisfaction and happiness, deserving or feeling entitled to satisfaction is another thing altogether.

Shifting the belief that one deserves and is entitled to sexual satisfaction often includes first the process of articulating its definition. Often, this provokes a discussion of how little discussion there has been so far about desires in a concrete manner. In these cases, a series of conversations and homework sessions designed to help the couple explore barriers to change can be undertaken. Sex therapists are accustomed to helping clients to define and to strive toward sexual satisfaction—and also to navigate sexual frustrations. There is also a need, however, to develop a sense of the needs of the other; a framework for mutuality; an understanding of moment-to-moment consent; a productive dialogue about sexual desires; and the capacity to tolerate disappointment. This usually leads to some emotion regulation and distress tolerance skills that are underdeveloped. In some cases, however, it becomes clear that the couple wishes to part ways, as they do not or cannot meet each other's sexual needs. Here is one example.

A couple that had been together for seven years and had always had problems in their relationship sexually wanted some help with navigating the issue. Neither of the partners had any difficulties with others previous to this relationship. They had difficulty being productive in discussions about their desires, however, and tended to launch into attacks ad hominem. Often he would approach her sexually and caress or kiss her or even verbally suggest that he was interested in sex. She would almost always brush him away physically and explain that he had approached her in the wrong way. He began to feel rejected and very despondent. He also felt mistreated and deserving of affection. She, on the other hand, felt very clear that she should not have to tolerate an unappealing approach.

What was most interesting is that he assumed from these exchanges that she wasn't interested in him. Because they were in a monogamous relationship, his hurt began to eventually shift to a sense of anger and then entitlement. He began to experience her as cold, frigid, and withholding. This fueled his sense of deserving and lack of care for her feelings. He felt shut out and hopeless. She, on the other hand, felt that his approach was insensitive but had not articulated thus far what would be a sensitive and acceptable approach in a way that he could understand. She felt that he should just know and that she shouldn't have to tell him how to behave. This was the area of focus for the first sessions.

In this case the clients had limited insight into their experiences and a lack of willingness to describe their desires. She could identify that she did not appreciate the particular approach or quality of touch but was unable to articulate (without prompting) if it was the timing of the approach, the pressure of the touch, the scriptedness of the events, or what other quality was objectionable. Through supporting her to get curious about what exactly was objectionable and what would be better, she was able to articulate that it wasn't the quality of his touch but that it felt intrusive and often ill timed. This led to a discussion of what could constitute the right time. As we unfolded these layers it became clear that she felt any approach was objectionable because it was linked psychologically to her history of sexual abuse that was somehow being triggered in these engagements at this time. A referral to an individual therapist for treatment of the trauma and their understanding of the events as linked to a larger issue helped to assuage some of his sense of deserving and hurt and also helped to put into context the infidelity that had occurred previously and brought them into therapy against the backdrop of her trauma.

Once the trauma was being processed in individual work, her sense of trust and desire resumed. She was able to find words to describe the kinds of contact she wanted, to allow her desires, and to allow his approach—and even to make her own approaches.

There is a potential relationship between entitlement and narcissism. Sometimes infidelity is driven by and supported by Narcissistic

Personality Disorder, narcissistic features, or even a newly defined phenomenon, sexual narcissism, which is defined by narcissism but restricted only to the sexual realm (Widman & McNulty, 2014). In these cases, to change the perception of deservingness and entitlement in the one who has an affair is less possible because it is a more pervasive and deeply rooted perspective. In this case, the infidelity can be seen as a symptom of narcissism and the treatment goals should be to address the underlying narcissism through individual depth-oriented psychotherapy. Clear assessment of the extent of narcissistic features and capacity for flexibility, change, and empathy is important in treatment planning. In the case discussed earlier in this section, the entitlement was a function of ongoing frustration and a felt sense of unfairness restricted to this particular relationship, not a case of narcissism that was more pervasive, so it was somewhat easy to change. There are a number of cases of infidelity that are fueled by a more significant set of personality characteristics, however. These types of cases and others that have comorbid psychopathology should be handled with those symptoms in mind rather than treated only as cases of infidelity.

The Partner and the Self Are Viewed as Fixed Characters

This is an interesting issue. The entire enterprise of psychotherapy is predicated on the idea that people can and do change and through these changes come to experience more satisfying relationships. Psychotherapy also is based on the idea that change occurs through corrective relationships, most notably psychotherapeutic ones. If the therapist at the outset aligns consciously or unconsciously with the idea that either party is inherently less or more sexual or inherently good or bad in some way, then the idea that there is a fixed quality to either partner will be reinforced. Helping clients to experience the other as developing and creative is critical, and in particular helping couples to experiment with changes that may impact their sex lives is critical. There are of course cases where there are more fixed traits than others, as in personality disorders, personality traits, and defenses due to trauma or rigidity, or that there are irreconcilable differences, and in these cases deep work or parting ways may eventually be the logical solution. These decisions are often met more easily and the grief addressed if one has made a good effort to explore the malleability of the characters and their perceptions to accommodate the needs of both. And this requires that the needs and barriers to meeting them are articulated and confronted.

This particular constituent is critical to address, as it represents an existential issue that we all face—the closing off of options and limitedness of time that we can experience more poignantly if our partner appears to be unchangeable. This particular quality of perceiving the other and self as fixed reinforces the dissatisfaction and hopelessness and the sense of desire for novelty and passion. The couple is in a perceptual rut and the life is drained from the relationship unless the subjectivity of the self and other can be fully embraced as a living, developing entity capable of play and novelty and surprise. We must encounter our vitality and choices as moving and alive in order to change this perception. Often this is best accomplished within therapy in vivo.

One interesting intervention to employ here is to consider with couples the barriers to change toward a more satisfying experience and to view the stated barriers as not actual barriers but rather as derivatives of the beliefs that prevent flexibility. An example would be that one party says that they never orgasm during partner sex and they resent having to satisfy the other only to have to masturbate to orgasm afterward. The other may say that they resent having to deal with the partner who is somewhat difficult to bring to orgasm. While these may be experienced as actual barriers, they also highlight the psychological rules that are at play that can be questioned. For example, beneath such a statement could be the idea that we are supposed to take care of the other person's orgasm or that partner sex includes the necessity to reach orgasm, or that there is something shameful about masturbation or that sexual acts must be mutually satisfying each time. Further, there could be some sexual skills to develop to enhance the possibility of orgasm occurring earlier or during partner sex. There are plenty of problematic beliefs about sex and relationships that people hold that keep them stuck. Rob Fisher (2002) has an excellent methodology for helping couples in particular, but it can also be applied to individuals, for assigning experiential activities for homework designed to help facilitate exploration and movement through confronting perceived barriers to change. Often these experiments bring people in contact with additional barriers or help them break through barriers, but in either case they serve to develop a more nuanced understanding and also facilitate movement and change and therefore vitality. As one partner sees the other change, the fixed perceptions are challenged. Here is an example.

Therapist: Describe to me the issues you think the two of you are having.

A: I am just more into sex. It's that simple. And I can't keep pestering her for it. We just are different. And that's OK, but if all I get to do is curb my desires and wait around it's really frustrating. Porn helps a bit but she's really judgmental about that too.

B: I don't think it's that at all. I just want her to not be so direct. She can't just come at me like that! What about getting me in the mood or something?

A:	But it takes so much and usually you don't get there anyway.
B:	If you would try for more than five minutes maybe I would?
Therapist:	So, it seems that one of you thinks these differences are innate and fixed and the other is proposing that there is a different way to approach that might result in something different happening?
B:	Yes, I need a different approach. But she isn't capable of it. She's like a bull in a china shop. And she's ready all the time. I don't think she's got any patience and I'm just not built like that!
Therapist:	Can you articulate what an idealized version of the approach you would like would be?
B:	Yes, it would include room for me to respond (gesturing a push away from her chest with both hands). I need time to take in what is happening and to experience it and see how I feel and sometimes I am all tied up in my head and it just takes time, you know?
Therapist:	(Noticing A rolling her eyes) What is it like when you are waiting for a response in these moments?
A:	It's exasperating. I am afraid that I will get shut down again and it all feels so pointless and frustrating. I can never do it right.
Therapist:	Hmmm. So there is a difference sometimes these days in terms of how quickly each of you can get into your body in the moment and participate in what is happening fully. What if you have to stay engaged for a bit longer to wait for her to get out of her head? What if it takes five more minutes or ten or fifteen sometimes?
A:	How will I know that she ever will get out of her head?
Therapist:	You could ask her, for example. Or you could agree to try for twenty minutes to see what the outer edge of that time is like.
A:	Hmm. I suppose. . . . Would that work?
B:	It could certainly make it clear that we were still trying to connect sexually and were willing to make space for me to catch up. I would appreciate that.
Therapist:	It would require that you tolerate not knowing for a bit of time if you will be rebuffed or not. And perhaps that would go better, I imagine, if you were reassured by her. Do you think you might be able to reassure her that you are working on getting out of your head and being in the moment so that she can stay engaged and not feel worried about a rejection?
B:	Sure. That's easy.
Therapist:	So, that's your homework this week and we'll discuss when you come back next week. Keep in mind that you can choose

> to do the work or not but in either case I will ask about it and in particular to ask about your observations of your thoughts and feelings and sensations whether you do it or not, about the homework assignment.

In this case, making clear that there are not fixed characters but instead a cycle that reifies the understanding of the characters as fixed is important. Then finding ways to demonstrate their desires to stay engaged is important. Oftentimes the issue of being out of sync in time and space is at the root of the perception of each of the characters being fixed. The context and approach are fixed and therefore the result is fixed. Changing some of these variables (e.g. how and when the approach for sex occurs) and helping them to not give up too soon is helpful in this case. Also experiments can be a great way to test beliefs. Sometimes people feel safer doing an experiment that the therapist suggests rather than approaching one another without a structure.

Lack of Curiosity for the Partner as a Subject

Several theorists have discussed the importance of a curious interested gaze facilitating development of erotic feelings (Halling, 2008; Perel, 2007; Schnarch, 2009). The ability for us to look across the room and see our partner as if for the first time as a person in his or her own right, as a subject with the potential for many different future acts and thoughts, is what often animates curiosity, interest, and sometimes attraction and eroticism. This gaze often includes empathy, affection, and warmth as we realize that the other is a subject, just as we are. We begin to have the experience of thinking about them, holding them in mind, through the gaze. These feelings fade when we cease being curious and think we know already who they are as a fixed entity and therefore have no need to gaze deeply.

Helping couples to consider the perspective of the other from a curious open stance as if they do not already know what the other feels is important. This can be done by modeling curiosity for the couple and exposing their assumptions. This is done so that they too come to learn something new about how they view their partner as a fixed entity and so that they might rekindle their original interest. Often this is a core skill that couples therapists support regardless of their approach. The therapist using non-judgmental curious language about all aspects of the discussions is a vital process to model. Modeling non-judgmental and empathic language serves to humanize very difficult aspects of infidelity and can help soften the dynamic and lead to a curious gaze or view of the other.

For example, therapist responses can come from a descriptive and curious stance devoid of inherent meanings. If the therapist assumes no malintent and does not ascribe to any particular explanation but remains curious, the clients also often follow suit in some ways, opening up to more possibilities. Usually, when the details of an affair are revealed in session therapists tend to align with and make empathic statements that support the feelings of the one who was betrayed about the actual affair. This is done in order to facilitate empathy for the other and to settle the upset in the room. This approach, however, is predicated on the idea that the one who had the affair does not require empathic support to untangle his or her feelings. A counterintuitive approach is to also humanize the perspectives of the one who had the affair and to get curious about the ways in which the person who was betrayed may have experienced the events prior to the affair. This can help to soften the belief that there was some malintent and can highlight the problematic ways that the dilemma came to be.

Statements to the betrayed may be like, "So, it must have really been hard for you to articulate your desires if you had been so shamed in your family about sexuality!" or "I can see how much you wanted to connect with him but also didn't want to fail him" or "It must have been so confusing and difficult to find time to connect when there was such distance." Statements to the one who had the affair might be more like, "I can really see how troubling it must have been to want to connect sexually, to feel like it was hopeless and see no possible solution" or "Wow, I really see how important it was for you to connect and how sad you were that it felt impossible to do so within the relationship and how much you wanted to remain in the relationship. It was a real dilemma!" or "I really get how difficult this has been" or "I can see how much you cared about remaining romantically and sexually engaged with your husband but you also didn't want to push the issue. In a way you were trying to be respectful by not raising the issue." Each of these types of statements can help the couple to soften their judgments and get curious about the experience of the other and to get beyond the blame that often dominates therapy for infidelity. Often this kind of discussion feels more affirming and soothing and leads to an apology that is full and more likely to be received rather than a forced apology and defensiveness.

A note about developing the curious gaze that leads to erotic feelings: The gaze is predicated on some amount of differentiation and distance. Sometimes returning to what is structurally often present in courtship (e.g. having separate hobbies and interests and time apart and investing in adventures and substantive conversations) can facilitate more of the desire and longing and curiosity that fuels sexual and romantic energy and also a respect for subjectivity of the other (Perel, 2007). Working on attending to differentiation as a process can be important in development of empathy and curiosity as well as eroticism.

An Experience of Desire and Passion Overriding
and Overtaking One's Judgment

We have all been primed for this through movies and books where the arc of the story includes the heroic narrative and romantic scenes. We are not particularly adept at understanding in real time our sensations, feelings, and intentions in a logical manner and in fact even romanticize the idea that we can be swept off our feet by some magical passionate encounter by an idealized other. We even come to see the idea of passionate experiences to imply that there is something more important happening than if we had access to our deliberative qualities during these erotic moments. This allows us to privilege the feelings rather than to consider our decisions and makes way for affairs occurring without much consideration and deliberation. In fact the passion and excitement of the beginning of an affair together with this particular belief even serves to justify the experience of infidelity when sex lives are lackluster.

Mindfulness exercises can be very helpful for developing the capacity to notice sensations, feelings, thoughts, and other aspects of internal life more readily so that we might notice in real time and choose in real time how to proceed or not in ways that take into account the multilayered experience of passion and ethical issues that coexist the moment an affair is born. Helping people to discern choice points requires that they are mindful of their experiences in each moment as time passes. Borrowed from Dialectical Behavioral Therapy (DBT) (Linehan, 1993) is the idea of using mindfulness to reflect on the thoughts, feelings, behaviors, and sensations that occur to develop skills for regulating and noticing the choice points that we all have all the time. While Linehan (1993) applied these techniques to helping those with Borderline Personality Disorder to address problematic behaviors (e.g. suicidal thoughts, cutting, angry outbursts), they can also be applied to any powerful emotional experience that we wish to navigate, such as passion. Noticing the choice points we all have when feeling strongly is important in making decisions we do not later regret. I won't digress here to deliver a discussion of DBT skills work or the larger field of mindfulness-based techniques; however, helping those who have experienced passion sweep them away without much recognition of the choice points that lead up to the infidelity and to anticipate the likely regret and impact of their actions is important. Also helping people to understand erotic experiences, flirting, and other sensations and experiences from a mindful perspective is often helpful. This process includes developing awareness of thoughts, feelings, sensations, behaviors, and impulses so that they can be engaged in an integrated manner more directly. This is likely the best approach to "affair prevention" in that it helps people to experience more consciously the experiences and choices that precede affairs rather than other approaches that include others monitoring the behavior of the one who cheated.

In addition, the field of sex therapy has much to offer by way of helping couples to develop passion and novelty within their relationships. With some direction and investment often couples who are willing can develop eroticism and novelty through new experiences together. Sometimes they simply need some direction and support or need help with processing their concerns about new sexual acts and erotic energy in order to proceed.

The Affair Is Not Recognized as an Affair Until After It Begins

Many people are genuinely surprised themselves that they end up in affairs. They don't start out with intentions to hurt anyone or to engage in infidelity. They are not aware that it is problematic until after it has already occurred. It is painful to reconcile that there is a set of desires that can never be met in either relationship so they seem to make an alternate narrative. Again, this is not deliberate or with malicious intent. This goes back to Freud suggesting that sexual and aggressive impulses are often buried within the unconscious so that we may remain polite and navigate a civilized society easily. This same set of forces also makes it difficult to remain connected to the aggressive hostility toward the spouse or partner and sexual feelings that can occur with others at times and to continue to live politely and civilly. Helping people to understand consciously their anger toward their partner and their sexual desires that are unmet as natural and normal parts of being human often helps people to understand how they "fell into" an affair and also helps them to become aware of these potentialities later. What is most interesting about couples that experience infidelity is that often they are poor at arguing and tend toward being nicey-nicey with one another. When asked if they have discussed the depth of despair that one has about feeling sexually or romantically neglected, often they have not discussed this deeply or often enough and certainly have not argued extensively about it, or, if they have, the one who is feeling desperate has not made it completely clear that he or she or they is hopeless about how the relationship can move forward for a wide variety of reasons. Couples often avoid making the most important point, which is that they see no way to solve the dilemma and don't want to divorce and need help to figure this out. Couples that cannot or do not metabolize their anger toward one another and also do not discuss their sexual feelings find these remain underground and unconsciously present only to arise in another form, often evoked when an attractive other presents.

Sometimes the lack of sexual connection and erotic tension is not even present to couples at all. They subscribe to the idea that all long-term relationships are boring or devoid of sexual excitement over time and are not even aware that they are missing something, so arguing about the depth of this loss is not possible. What sometimes brings it into consciousness is the strong felt attraction to another. Only with hindsight then can the couple come to understand that there have been parts of their experience that are suppressed—the loss and the desire.

Regardless, working with loss and desire is a critical issue in therapy for infidelity. Existential-humanistic approaches are well-positioned to address these concerns, but a great number of other theoretical orientations also are relevant for grief and frustrated desires. It is merely that the therapist must conceptualize the treatment not as infidelity but instead as grief and loss.

Divorce or Opening Up the Relationship Are Not Considered Options for Resolving the Issues

These are not people who wish to be in conflict with their spouse and they also don't really want to leave or open up the relationship, per se. They seem to fear the consequences of disrupting what they have at all costs by really exploring any of these options. Making these structural options clearer may help the couple confront the issues or at the very least may make it perfectly clear that there is a crisis brewing. Certainly, making sure not to be biased against any of these options is important for clinicians both from an ethical standpoint and because sometimes the way out of the dilemma is a structural solution. Ironically, asking couples to consider their reasons for staying together or their reasons for wanting monogamy, at the right moments of therapy, can have helpful clarifying effects, making the choices transparent and therefore the idea that they have a choice at all! Also sometimes there is a rubber band effect in asking these questions. If we ask why not divorce, couples often begin to talk about all the reasons they wish to stay together, which is helpful for them to hear and often causes them to feel a stronger attachment. To truly understand the dilemma requires at some point that we unpack the structural options to solving the dilemma, thus confronting the issue of choice as opposed to avoidance. It may support a renewed commitment to monogamy or may offer other avenues for integrity (e.g. a negotiated open relationship or divorce) or a deeper level of exploration of the current issues.

The same issue of bias that therapists tend to have against divorce or opening up their relationships is mirrored in the general population. While divorce can have significant repercussions and should not be the first consideration, there are also many cases of those who divorce and have happy subsequent lives. Similarly, open relationships are difficult to negotiate and manage and are not for everyone, and yet many people live very happily in these types of structures. These considerations would also be structural solutions to the dilemmas that would relieve the stress within the relationships and would not necessitate lying or cheating—one of the core defining elements of an affair.

An example follows that illustrates the possibilities of successfully resolving the dilemma with an open relationship structure. It also illustrates some of the ways in which technology can impact a couple.

> A thirty-something queer couple who had been together for two and a half years came in to discuss their lack of connection and in particular their lack of sexual connection. While they both enjoyed the sex they had, she wanted more frequent sex and more engaged passionate sex. When she approached him, usually he would be preoccupied with work or otherwise unavailable. "Maybe later," he would often say. She would get more and more frustrated as the days and weeks would go by and they would have sex a few times a month but he was still often preoccupied. She finally brought him to sex therapy because she was considering breaking up or suggesting the need to open up their relationship. She didn't want to leave him but also wanted to have more frequent and passionate sex and saw him as inherently unable to deliver on this point. She felt that she would be able to satisfy this urge outside their relationship without much jealousy or conflict and she wasn't sure how he would react or how to set up such an arrangement so that it would be successful.
>
> During the initial appointments it was clear they loved each other and clear that they wanted to work this out if possible. In assessing their sexual histories, it also became clear that they had a typical desire discrepancy, with him generally feeling less desire for partner sex and her feeling more. In addition, while he could easily get erect, he required more time than her to "get in the mood" for passionate lovemaking. He found it difficult to transition from his all-consuming work and needed some time to connect with her in a deep conversation before engaging in sex in order to feel comfortable and present. He knew he was disappointing her, and yet their busy lives were very full and he didn't have the time and space to make sex a priority.
>
> He would also often watch porn during the day (he worked from home as a consultant), sometimes for many hours, while she was away at work. He felt a great deal of shame about this not only because of the amount of time he would spend but also because of the types of porn he was watching. He noted that it didn't start out that way. Usually he would be working and would feel bored and would find himself distracted with shopping online or paying bills or whatever, and then he would get lost searching for something, reading something, and eventually he would say that he would end

up watching porn. Once he began watching he found himself surfing from porn site to site searching for "the end of the Internet," he would say, always trying to find something more salacious or novel or more interesting than what he typically found. The searching is what would take so much time and all the while that he would search he would masturbate but not to climax. Only when he found something that he thought was sufficiently interesting would he allow himself to finally climax and get back to his work. The entire cycle was exhausting and very time consuming and generally unsatisfying.

We considered as a group that perhaps there might be a link between his relatively low desire for partner sex and his porn use and masturbatory habits. At the same time he was deeply ashamed and unable to discuss his habits in much detail in couples therapy. She wanted full disclosure about what he was finding ultimately compelling and was worrying that he didn't find her attractive. In a couples context both were reactive and were heading into a constant triggering state, with his withholding triggering her feelings of insecurity and her insecurity fueling her demands for his disclosure of his porn, which triggered his shame, and the cycle would continue.

Eventually with a few meetings individually, he was able to map the antecedent and consequence of all the decision points in his porn sessions and to bring more awareness to how he uses technology and where all the decision points are in the process. He quickly was able to decide to limit his use to three times a week during scheduled times (one hour each) and found other outlets for boredom and refocusing. This left him feeling more in control of his time and better able to approach his girlfriend with sexual desire. Because he felt less shame, we were able to process the fantastical elements of porn that he found interesting and to demystify porn for them both. He was having satisfying sex with his partner and felt proud to be in control, so a full disclosure of what he was watching became less shameful and less triggering for them. When he finally did disclose what he was watching, and it was less mainstream but nothing objectionable from a forensic standpoint, there was less of a trigger for her because she was getting what she needed through their partner sex and was feeling desired. Similarly, in individual sessions we were able to consider the relationship between boredom and fantasy and how porn fills this particular need for him. Had we begun from the place of full disclosure or stayed in a couples format, we may have stayed stuck and shame would have been omnipresent.

The phenomenological findings suggest that the constituents underlie the infidelity and should be addressed through treatment at some point. Because perceptions can be changed to open up more possibilities for development and growth, it is suggested that therapy for infidelity specifically target these problematic perceptions that reinforce one another and give rise to the possibilities of infidelity occurring and that underpin the experience. A more complete set of exercises and activities for clinicians is presented to further explore how this approach can be helpful.

Notes

1 There are a great number of decision-making scenarios that have been documented in cognitive and social psychological research, for example, that suggest that we are not always adept at anticipating risk and often fall prey to regret (Slovic, 2000; Gilovich, Griffen & Kahneman, 2002; Kahneman, 2012). In the case of the phenomenon of infidelity, it is often not experienced as a single decision to act at one point in time; it is instead the sum total of many small acts and choices that add up to an experience that isn't recognized as the decision to have an affair at the time (Owen, Rhoades, & Stanley, 2013) in the same way that smoking a single cigarette isn't encountered as a decision to become a smoker because one cannot accurately anticipate how one might feel after starting to smoke (Slovic, 2000; Zapien, 2016). This is why the beginning of an affair may occur at a moment in time but is more often later understood as a series of moments sliding toward fate.

2 There are a great number of theorists who have attempted to settle the issue of nature and nurture and sexual desire (Ryan & Jetha, 2011; Foucault, 1990). There are solid arguments that support biological determinism; gender differences in the experiences of sexuality; and social constructivist views of the very issues of gender, desire, and so on. We have reasons to critique the epistemological issues with our study of sexuality and to consider the ways in which we both affirm and reify many of these beliefs through the production of research through the design. Critical views of determinism suggest that gender, desire, and eroticism change and are fluid and that there is a much wider range of experiences and possible experiences available to all of us. The clinician is wise to hold all of these possibilities at the same time and to help our clients to investigate their multifaceted experiences in an attempt to transcend any and all limitations that reside in a single viewpoint.

3 In cases of erectile dysfunction is it important to make sure that clients have had a recent check-up with their physician, as high blood pressure can result in ED and sometimes this can be an important indicator of a possible impending cardiac event. At the same time, while ED can be treated with medications and likely a physician will recommend this because it addresses the ED symptoms, ED can also be treated with sex therapy and psychotherapy without pharmacological intervention. Because there are side effects to the medications and often men feel less self-esteem when they rely on them, it is ideal to suggest behavioral interventions first if possible, with a sex therapist in particular. A referral for a check-up is necessary regardless in these cases. If possible, careful consideration of the meaning clients make of medications and the referrals in these contexts is important.

References

American Psychiatric Association. (2013). *Diagnostic and Statistical Manual—5th edition*. Washington, DC: APA.

Bordin, E. (1979). The generalizability of the psychoanalytic concept of the working alliance. *Psychotherapy: Theory, Research and Practice*, 16(3), pp. 252–260.

Braun-Harvey, M., & Vigorito, M. (2016). *Treating Out of Control Sexual Behavior: Rethinking Sex Addiction*. New York, NY: Springer.

Fisher, R. (2002). *Experiential Psychotherapy with Couples: A Guide for the Creative Pragmatist*. New York, NY: Zeig, Tucker & Theisen.

Foucault, M. (1990). *The History of Sexuality: An Introduction*. New York, NY: Random House.

Gilovich, T., Griffen, D., & Kahneman, D. (2002). *Heuristics and Biases: The Psychology of Intuitive Judgment*. New York, NY: Cambridge University Press.

Giorgi, A. (2009). *The Descriptive Phenomenological Method in Psychology: A Modified Husserlian Approach*. Pittsburgh, PA: Duquesne University Press.

Glass, S. (2003). *Not "Just Friends": Rebuilding Trust and Recovering Your Sanity After Infidelity*. New York, NY: Simon & Schuster.

Halling, S. (2008). *Intimacy, Transcendence and Psychology*. New York, NY: Palgrave Macmillan.

Horvath, A. (2005). The therapeutic relationship: Research and theory. *Psychotherapy Research*, 15(1–2).

Horvath, A., & Greenberg, L. (2005). *The Working Alliance: Theory, Research and Practice*. San Francisco, CA: Wiley Publishers.

Horvath, A., & Symonds, D. (1991). Relation between working alliance and outcome in psychotherapy: A meta-analysis. *Journal of Counseling Psychology*, 38(2), pp. 139–149.

Kahneman, D. (2012). *Thinking Fast and Slow*. New York, NY: Farrar, Strauss and Giroux.

Linehan, M. (1993). *Cognitive-Behavioral Treatment of Borderline Personality Disorder*. New York, NY: Guillford Press.

Morin, J. (1996). *The Erotic Mind*. New York, NY: Harper Perennial.

Owen, J., Rhoades, G., & Stanley, S. (2013). Sliding versus deciding in relationships: Associations with relationship quality, commitment and infidelity. *Journal of Couples and Relationship Therapy*, 12(2), pp. 135–149.

Perel, E. (2007). *Mating in Captivity: Unlocking Erotic Intelligence*. New York, NY: Harper Collins.

Ryan, C., & Jetha, C. (2011). *Sex at Dawn: How We Mate, Why We Stray, and What It Means for Modern Relationships*. New York, NY: Harper Collins.

Schnarch, D. (2009). *Passionate Marriage: Keeping Love and Intimacy Alive in Committed Relationships*. New York, NY: Norton and Co.

Slovic, P. (2000). *The Perception of Risk*. New York, NY: Earthscan.

Stalfa, F., & Hastings, C. (2005). "Accusatory Suffering" in the offended spouse. *Journal of Couple and Relationship Therapy*, 4(2/3), p. 83.

Widman, L., & McNulty, J. (2014). Sexual narcissism and infidelity in early marriage. *Archives of Sexual Behavior*, 43(7), pp. 1315–1325.

Zapien, N. (2016). The beginning of an extra-marital affair: A phenomenological study and clinical implications. *Journal of Phenomenological Psychology*, 47(2), p. 134.

Chapter 7

Clinical Skills Development and Practical Application

Practical application of these ideas follows in the next section in two forms. In the first, there is a sample case complete with treatment planning suggestions for the entire arc of treatment taken from composite actual cases. This is offered as an example that can inform a wide range of client situations and circumstances related to infidelity but is designed to illustrate how the phenomenological structure informs assessment and treatment. Thereafter, a series of reflective exercises, readings, and other resources are presented to help facilitate reflection and growth for the clinician based on what has been discovered through the research findings discussed in the previous chapters. These exercises are designed to help the interested clinician to reflect and build capacity to address infidelity and sexuality more broadly in an intentional manner and to provide ways to engage more deeply with the issue. The reader can work through these activities and sources as you wish in any order. It is my hope that these exercises and discussions are practical and immediately applicable and serve the public and your clients.

The Case of Tammy and Larry

Tammy and Larry have been married for eight years and together for thirteen years. They met in college and had a tumultuous relationship and were often undecided and ambivalent about whether or not they were well-matched. They broke up and got back together many times before finally deciding to live together and marry. Other than this particular and confusing recurring conflict they rarely argued and seemed to be a very happy couple. Larry was a very cerebral person and somewhat soft-spoken. He adored his wife and felt very proud with her by his side. Sometimes he could not understand her emotions, moods, and needs, however. She would be happy and joyful and very expressively so sometimes and other times would be quite despondent and dark and often he did not fully understand why. For him these kinds of extreme feelings do not occur, and when he does feel strongly about something he is not particularly demonstrative about it. His understanding of the situation is that this is because she is a woman and he believes that women feel and think differently than men about a great number of issues. He assumes this is a normal point of confusion and disconnection for heterosexual couples.

Tammy feels that he is limited in his expressiveness and ability to be creative and inspired and passionate. Their sex life prior to therapy was fine for him but really lacking for her. It was technically skillful and both experienced desire, arousal, and orgasm regularly. They had intercourse at least weekly but sometimes more frequently for most of their marriage, but for Tammy there simply wasn't much passion or novelty. They had several conversations about this, always initiated by Tammy. He usually responded defensively and with confusion and then nothing changed. She wanted more drama, more engagement, more feeling, more dynamism, more play. In short, she wanted more vitality in the relationship, like an opera, or a melodrama, or like one sees in foreign films sometimes, she noted. They came to therapy because he found her in bed with a neighbor unexpectedly when he came home from work sick one day. He averted his eyes, told the neighbor to get out or he'd kill him, and has spoken very little to Tammy since. It has been five days since this incident.

Tammy called to initiate couples therapy because after the discovery, in his silence and brooding, he has been avoiding her and she fears that the relationship is over. She does not want to continue the affair and also finds the quiet and distance she is experiencing from her husband to be intolerable. She is panicked.

Therapist Reflections

Among the first issues to address are what the unit of treatment is to be and what the goals of therapy might become. While Tammy is suggesting couples therapy, this is only possible if Larry is willing. Ascertaining the degree to which Larry is willing can be done by asking Tammy to invite Larry, but it is preferred to have a short call with each individually to determine the perspective of each party on the issues and degree of willingness to participate. This can also help with treatment planning and to develop a sense of safety for each through development of an early therapeutic alliance that is balanced for each.

The next issue to address is building rapport and conceptualizing their treatment. It is a period of assessment. For her there is a felt sense of worry because he is not speaking to her. She is motivated to seek therapy because of her discomfort and worry that she has lost her husband. The other issues (e.g. the feelings and context that made possible the affair) are somewhat problematic for her to address at this juncture if she is motivated primarily to assuage his concerns and reassure herself that he is not leaving. Yet because of the research discussed earlier, a course of therapy designed to assuage her immediate concerns and build his trust will be insufficient. There is a need to do this first perhaps, but then to address what we can surmise might exist for her beneath the first set of feelings—the perceptions are the constituents of the phenomenon of infidelity—will become important. This is the part that is unique about this book and provides a new contribution.

It is likely that if Larry is motivated to come to couples therapy at all that he may have a different agenda for the sessions. He is likely shocked that this occurred and is devastated. He may not feel trusting of his wife and may want to address the issue of why this occurred quite directly so that he can make sense of the shock and upset. This may make the various disparate goals for therapy, at least initially, difficult. She needs to be soothed. He needs to understand and emote. He needs to feel trust. And she needs to reflect on how this occurred and process the perceptions that made this possible. It will be important for the therapist to meet with them together to see how they talk to one another and relate to one another with the other present so that he or she can sequence these goals and structure therapy. This will provide an initial view into the relational dynamics and communication styles. The therapist can identify strengths and weaknesses. Then a separate session with each to allow each to speak freely without the other present will offer a chance for gathering more information than can be had in a couples format in that there can be a full story without the reactivity of the other or the self-editing that often occurs when there is a dyad. Before doing so, it is recommended that you make the purpose of separate sessions very clear and discuss your secrets policy. This is particularly important so that in case any issues with triangulation or additional details about the affair(s) come up in these individual sessions, the therapist isn't in a problematic role relative to the secrets. It is possible that the affair is still going on or that there are feelings about the third party that may arise. Without a secrets policy the therapy can become problematic and can replicate the betrayal in many ways through the individual assessment sessions. Larry will be more likely to be forthcoming in this arrangement. And if there is a need to refer the parties out to individual therapy this can be assessed. The therapist can assess for underlying issues as well (e.g. substance use, sexual issues, psychopathology) and the perspective of each of the meaning of this event. After these sessions the therapist will have a better view of what to do next.

After a phone call with each, a couples session, and an individual session with each, all of which included open-ended non-judgmental curious questions designed to inform the goals and treatment planning, the following became clear. Larry did not have any complaints about their marriage until the affair was discovered. He was completely taken by surprise and deeply hurt and confused by this. The moods and desires for passion, emotion, and vitality that Tammy has made clear over the years have really been confusing for him and he has had no idea what to make of these complaints or discussions. He could be described as having very little range of emotion and limited emotional expression. He is a warm man, despite his relative reservedness, and is certainly thoughtful and loves her deeply. Introverted, shy, and pragmatic all are adjectives that describe Larry. At this point he does not seem to exhibit signs of autism spectrum disorder or language and communication issues that are pathological, although there is interest in understanding more about the couples' inability to communicate well. It is easy to imagine that Tammy, who is more expressive and social, might yearn for more engagement and demonstrativeness from him. For Larry, the response to Tammy's affair is simply shock, anger, and hurt, and it is experienced as an internal well of deep emotional blackness. He sees no way out of these feelings, no way to resolve them, no reason to express them, and also does not want to divorce his wife. He speaks very little to her because he is trying to figure out a way to solve this particular dilemma, and he has no substantive options yet so he remains silent. He could be characterized as depressed although not suicidal. He simply drifts from day to day with a broken heart trying to figure out how she could have done this with logical principles. He is not sure what therapy can do for him or them and hopes that there is a way to work it out.

Tammy, on the other hand, having been hurt by his lack of expression before the affair, now feels terribly anxious with his silence. She doesn't sleep or eat much. She worries constantly that she is a bad person and worries that she will lose him, which was not her intention. The affair has been going on for more than six months and she hadn't expected that he would find out. Somehow it existed in a separate part of her mind and addressed a need she has had, but she really kept it separate from her relationship because she loves Larry. It was a way for her to meet a need that felt critically important that she couldn't get him to fulfill and she thought he would never know. Now she feels awful and characterizes herself as selfish. His silence underscores her shame and moves her to pester him to talk, and this provides no solace or answers. She feels dreadful about hurting Larry and finds it difficult to concentrate on the original issues of disconnection in the marriage and their difficulties talking about these issues. She needs soothing and a plan to stabilize her marriage and to address her sense of shame and guilt.

Therapist Reflections

Larry could benefit from some individual therapy. He has very little insight into the nuances of his feelings or the dilemma that preceded the affair and the dilemma that remains in their marriage—he has a limited (from her perspective) range of emotionality and expressiveness, and they do not discuss or work through this issue in any productive manner. Development on behalf of Larry in this way would hopefully give rise to his ability to be more aware of and forthcoming with his inner experience and feelings and/or to understand her emotionality and needs. This would likely make a conversation more productive and might ease their dynamic. This will require, however, individual work to facilitate an understanding of her and his emotional lives.

As for Tammy, while couples work may be helpful to address the immediate issues of anxiety, trust, and fear, and Tammy likely needs this context to soothe her, Tammy could benefit from working through some of the other issues that are likely beneath the immediate crisis. We can surmise, per the phenomenological research findings, that Tammy felt hopeless and stuck in the marriage prior to the affair. She was ambivalent in college and often raised concerns that were unmet and misunderstood or even dismissed. We can also see how she can easily come to perceive that she has a greater inherent capacity for novelty and passion and has potentially come to feel entitled to have this in her sexual experiences. From her description of the affair with the neighbor we can tell that he is more expressive, playful, and passionate than her husband, and that this is why he was compelling against the deprivation she felt. The phenomenological model in this case could fit quite well and might guide treatment for her individually or within the couple. It would also address the longstanding underpinnings of the relationship that made possible the affair. Without attending to these, the work is incomplete and will leave room for accusatory suffering, ongoing worries, disappointment, guilt, and shame. These areas can become a focus in the individual work for Tammy.

However, if Larry is not particularly forthcoming or lacks the skills to access his emotions and insight in the couples session, attempting to shift the constituents that made possible the affair such as feelings of hopelessness or unmet desires for passion may be challenging to shift. These two sides must be addressed individually, and in couples in collaboration with the various therapists involved to impact the system optimally. Similarly, if Tammy only wants to connect with Larry because she feels his distance, she may find it difficult to also delve into the material that drove the affair in the first place. Building her capacity to self-soothe, tolerate difficult emotions, and stay in dialogue without worrying about abandonment is needed. In addition, working through any attachment issues or abandonment fears would also be helpful, as these seem to be related to her experiences with both Larry and the neighbor. It may be more helpful to address this part of the issue as well, in individual work with Tammy and in the couples work. In this case the work would focus on shifting the beliefs that she holds about novelty, sex, entitlement,

passion, and working toward building these aspects within the relation-
ship and shoring up her self-soothing and emotion tolerance capacities.
All of these goals may require individual therapy for each and couples
therapy as well.

After several couples sessions the couple is able to come to an understanding that they do not want to divorce and that they need time to
both process the affair but also the issues that we surmise underlie the
affair per the phenomenological findings. They are working in weekly
individual sessions and meeting every other week for couples sessions,
each with different therapists.[1] The therapists are collaborating on the
treatment goals and each is working to support individuation and insight
that can be used to fuel productive conversations in couples work. After
several months the affair itself recedes as a main focus. While it is still
painful to see the neighbor and it can be painful when the memories are
evoked, the work that Larry is doing to develop his ability to understand
and share his inner life and to be more playful with his wife is helping her
to feel closer to him and less stuck and less panicked. Tammy is working
on revising the idealized version of love and romance she often has and
developing more skillful ways to ask for what she does want and developing those desires herself within the relationship. Her emotion tolerance skills and self-soothing capacity is developing for when she doesn't
get her needs met. They may want to focus more squarely on sex and
passion in sessions now and are preparing to terminate therapy. They
are using the phenomenological constituents as considerations for what
might be underlying their original issues that fueled their early break-ups
and the affair. For long-term growth and development they are working
to consider and shift the ideas that fuel ambivalence and distance in the
relationship. The affair is viewed as a symptom now and not the problem
itself.

Therapist Notes

It can be important toward the end of therapy for the couples therapist
to meet with each individual again. This provides a chance for each per-
son to voice clearly what remains as problematic or as residue from the
affair. It is typical that sometimes it can seem in the couples sessions that
all is wonderful and there is little emphasis on discussing whatever might
still remain as concerns. The forces that made difficult the direct discus-
sion of the ambivalence and concerns originally may remain to a certain
extent, and this is best considered individually, as people are more likely
to reveal their concerns without the other present. This type of check-in
can provide a context for each to be asked if there are any issues that
remain or concerns that remain that gave rise to the affair. For Tammy,

it would be important to check to see if the progress they have made has shifted her views of her marriage. If she feels it is positive but insufficient, if they terminate therapy and later experience a series of difficult weeks and months, she is primed to take up her faulty beliefs again that Larry is fundamentally not a good match and that she is entitled to passion elsewhere. Confronting the possibility of residual beliefs is important, and shoring up her skills for driving the engagement or managing or confronting her ongoing beliefs is important. Specifically, teaching how to drive passion, engagement, novelty, and playfulness with supportive homework and activities in session is perhaps warranted so that it feels possible. Also, asking the difficult questions of whether or not this relationship ultimately will not satisfy is important so that the existential question of choice and limitedness are engaged. We do this not to suggest divorce, but so that at some point we engage the idea that when things are insufficient that there are several routes out of this dilemma—divorce, open up the relationship, accept the limitations, work on changing them, or cheat. We develop skills for acceptance and driving change so that they can choose which of these options is best and give the sense that there are choices made in advance through how we engage or fail to engage these existential issues. In the termination sessions of the couples work it is important to reinforce the changes they have made and provide some direction for ongoing development. Often it can be important to make it clear that development sometimes requires a tune-up or that there may be circumstances that are challenging, and some of the work will seem to backslide, and this doesn't imply that they have failed. Encouraging couples to remind themselves of the routes they took to improve things and that therapy can also be engaged again before there is a significant problem is important. Even priming them with a sense of what the warning signs might be—hopelessness, fantasies about others that are significant, etc.—that might suggest therapy is indicated again might be helpful. Once this is all accomplished, termination can ensue.

Tammy and Larry left the couples therapy work after two years. Through this work they became much closer and more able to discuss their inner lives. Tammy continues to be more extroverted and passionate and has taken charge of driving the kinds of sexual and erotic experiences she wishes to have despite the fact that originally she felt that if he really loved her he should approach her because he is the man. Her work to bring her understanding of her gender role and sexual feelings of worth together with her naturally extroverted personality helped her decide to stop waiting around for him to emote and approach her and instead to use some skills that she has to facilitate intimacy and desire. She has found that if she initiates play or sex or emotional discussions in a productive, receptive, non-demanding, inviting way, her more introverted husband participates freely and she is much more satisfied with their connection. While it is not perfect or an idyllic romanticized view of how she thought things should go, she is slowly feeling more and more satisfied and is dismantling the image of perfectly passionate romantic relationships as the only acceptable ideal.

From time to time Tammy runs into the neighbor and feels a tremendous mix of feelings—shame, guilt, fear, desire, and sadness. She feels a strong allegiance to her husband and knows that this man represents a great deal of pain for Larry. Yet, for Tammy, this man represents both pain and desire. He was very kind and passionate and fit in perfectly with her romantic ideals at that particular point in her marital discord. She has come to view the neighbor both as a person in his own right and as a symbolic stand-in for her faulty perceptions, and yet she did not mean to hurt him either through the affair or its end. She has not talked to him much after they were discovered and they broke the affair off. She wonders how he is doing and feels badly that this was how their relationship ended. She worries less, however, about this than her husband's feelings and building their relationship. She is trying to develop a sense of peace about the affair too in her ongoing individual work.

Larry, through the work, has grown more able to discern his feelings and desires and is now more willing to share them. While he may be more pragmatic than Tammy and is still fundamentally more cerebral and introverted, he is also developing and showing more of his opinions, feelings, and desires. Their sex has become more varied, playful, and fun, and they have taken up more hobbies and interests both individually and together. There is a sense of vitality and dynamism that is developing.

Larry prefers not to think about the affair. He is particularly upset when he is reminded of the affair, and sometimes if he is reminded he falls into a short period of darkness and withdraws. He is working on making peace with these feelings and he still sometimes finds it difficult to understand how she could have an affair and love him as she says she does. He sometimes fantasizes about moving or making a significant change to get away from the reminders of the neighbor, but they cannot yet afford to move. He also knows that moving won't erase the memories. He will continue to focus on this in individual work. In some ways he has made a great deal of progress on his grief.

Exercise #1

This activity is designed in order to consider directly the ways in which our experiences and the stories we have heard may impact our views about marriage, divorce, sexuality, and opening up. There are several texts that are recommended below for further reading about each of these in order to orient the reader to draw from a broader set of studies and ideas than their own experiences so that we might competently engage these topics from a client-centered perspective.

Consider your personal experiences with marriage, divorce, monogamy, poly relationships, swinging, open relationships, infidelity, and sexuality. Include also those experiences that have impacted you somewhat directly but that you have not experienced personally (e.g. relationships of parents or grandparents, friends, and community members) but also what you have heard from others, media you have consumed, and client stories you have taken in about these structures and experiences. Consider how these may have shaped your views. Do you know of anyone who has a "good marriage," has had a "good divorce," or has a "good open relationship"? Consider the messages you have received from your family, communities, and peers.

Exercise #2

The following includes some recommended texts that may be informative on some of the related issues to infidelity. Challenge yourself to become familiar with some of the key sexuality texts.

Anapol, D. (2010). *Polyamory in the 21st Century: Love and Intimacy With Multiple Partners*. Lanham, MD: Rowman & Littlefield Publishing.

Braun-Harvey, D., & Vigorito, M. (2016). *Treating out of Control Sexual Behavior: Rethinking Sex Addiction*. New York, NY: Springer.

Carrigan, M., Gupta, K., & Morrison, T. (2014). *Asexuality and Sexual Normativity: An Anthology*. New York, NY: Routledge.

Coontz, S. (2006). *Marriage, a History: How Love Conquered Marriage*. New York, NY: Penguin Group.

Easton, D., & Hardy, J. (2009). *The Ethical Slut: A Practical Guide to Polyamory, Open-Relationships and Other Adventures*. Berkeley, CA: Celestial Arts.

Hertlein, K., & Blumer, M. (2014). *The Couple and Family Technology Framework: Intimate Relationships in a Digital Age*. New York, NY: Routledge.

Love, P., & Robinson, J. (2000). *Hot Monogamy: Essential Steps to More Passionate and Intimate Lovemaking*. Self-Published.

Morin, J. (1996). *The Erotic Mind*. New York, NY: Harper Collins Publishing.

Perel, E. (2007). *Mating in Captivity: Unlocking Erotic Intelligence*. New York, NY: Harper Collins Publishing.

Piercy, F., Hertlein, K., & Wetchler, J. (2005). *The Handbook of the Clinical Treatment of Infidelity*. New York, NY: Routledge.

Schnarch, D. (2009). *Passionate Marriage: Keeping Love and Intimacy Alive in Committed Relationships*. New York, NY: Norton & Company.

Winks, C., & Semans, A. (2002). *The Good Vibrations Guide to Sex: The Most Complete Sex Manual Ever*. Jersey City, NJ: Cleis Press.

Exercise #3

We reflect on content knowledge in key realms related to our therapeutic practice in order to identify areas within which we are competent to practice or to identify areas that we should ethically refer to other clinicians. In most communities, the Department of Public Health and several non-profits and for-profit sex education workshop providers offer the necessary and up-to-date information about sexuality to professionals.

Consider your ideas about sexual desire, sexual response, and sexual behavior. How did you learn about these areas? How relevant is your knowledge about sex to a broader group of people than yourself? In what areas, if any, do you think you perhaps have gaps in your knowledge?[2]

Exercise #4

It is important that psychotherapists have accurate information about sexuality and that they know their scope of practice when providing psychotherapy and do not overstep into sex education or sex therapy if they are not competent or trained. Often we do not know what we do not know, and many psychotherapists have been known to reinforce faulty beliefs about sex that are gender-biased or outdated. In reflecting upon our content knowledge or lack thereof, we come to appreciate the benefit of additional training or a referral for our clients' best interests.

What follows are some organizations that provide information that is considered comprehensive, up-to-date, medically accurate, and sex-positive to a great extent. While some clients may have religious or other values that conflict with a sex-positive inclusive perspective, such a perspective is useful because it provides complete information that otherwise is omitted or presented as immoral or unsavory relative to the religious views in question. Visit these sites to see what is available to inform your understanding of sexuality, desire, and related phenomena and you can choose then to filter these ideas in service of each client as needed.

www.aasect.org
www.goodvibes.com
www.guttmacher.org
www.hhs.gov
www.plannedparenthood.org
www.scarleteen.com
www.siecus.org

Exercise #5

We try to encounter that which might be more challenging to support in anticipation that we may encounter these scenarios in our clients and because there are people who are happy and healthy who engage in all of these structures.

Imagine a relationship structure that is different than the structure that you tend to prefer—choose a structure that you think would be the most difficult for you to affirm. For example, if you tend to find monogamy comforting and are challenged to see poly structures as tenable, then imagine a poly relationship structure more concretely. Once you have identified a more challenging arrangement consider how it might be healthy. What would be required to consider it healthy? Would different skills be necessary? Would this structure require different boundaries or ethics? What concerns do you have? How would the clinical endeavor need to shift to affirm such a structure? Are there assumptions that would need to be reconsidered that are embedded within clinical work with couples if you take this new perspective?

Exercise #6

We consider this in advance because many therapists are awkward at first when they begin to consider asking about sexuality. Some seem to get shy and self-conscious with the language, and others have not thought about the myriad issues that occur when considering timing, the therapeutic alliance, and putting the client at ease. Role-playing sessions can be very helpful to make this smoother.

Consider how easy or difficult it may be for you to bring up the topic of sexuality with clients and what language you might use. What concerns do you have, if any, about taking about sex? Do you imagine that there are situations when it might be difficult, problematic, or upsetting to raise the issue? How might you do so? When in the therapy? What are the benefits and drawbacks of raising the issue of sexuality in therapy?

Exercise #7

Often sex therapists or those who work with infidelity encounter sexual stories from our clients that are arousing or alternatively objectionable and disgusting to us personally. It can be very challenging in these situations unless there are skillfully employed and practiced strategies for metabolizing the erotic or revulsion countertransference reactions. Sex therapists have discovered that making sure to arrive to work feeling satisfied and aware of one's sexual self is important. It is also important to be clear and boundaried about one's role relative to clients' erotic material.

How does one manage erotic feelings in psychotherapy? Consider how it might be for you to become either aroused or disgusted by what a client describes about his or her sexual experiences. What skills can you employ so that you can remain present in discussions of sexuality and sexual fantasy and also stay focused on your clinical role? What for you might come up in such situations? How do you manage or feel about your own arousal or disgust? Some suggestions include: Seeking supervision, changing the topic at key intervals to guide the conversation toward what is clinically important, placing your attention on different aspects of the material (e.g. client emotions, observations of the client's somatic responses during session), or writing process notes. What for you might be helpful? And how does your own management of your erotic feelings differ, if at all, from managing hunger or tiredness in the clinical encounter?

Exercise #8

There are many views on these issues, and it is important for clinicians to develop some ideas about the relationship between eroticism and passion and context in order to be able to help our clients find ways to feel less hopeless. We do not usually have adequate information in our training to support this.

What are the ways in which attraction and desire develop between people? What forces do you imagine make attraction and desire, which were present previously, wane? What are the conditions now or in the past that have helped to facilitate desire and passion and intimacy for you? What are the conditions that make it wane? In what ways do you imagine you differ from others? What do you know about others' experiences? What are your beliefs about how desire may change in menopause or in older adults? How do you understand phenomena like asexuality, hypoactive desire disorder, or hyperactive desire disorder?

Exercise #9

Sex therapists and CBT- or DBT-oriented therapists often use activities designed to facilitate shifts in behavior, thoughts, or beliefs. In cases of infidelity and in working with the phenomenological constituents, which are beliefs, these approaches can be helpful. Consider experimenting with assigning your clients homework with the goal of using homework to discover how their particular internal landscape and relationship dynamics are organized. Homework is a way to facilitate discovery and sometimes is also a great intervention. In all cases, if you offer homework exercises, make sure that clients know they are optional but also are suggested so that they may mindfully encounter either the exercise or the resistance to the exercise—both are valuable. Some examples of homework include: Directed fantasies, exercises designed to develop eroticism in couples, exercises that develop skills to have constructive conflicts, directed porn consumption, or abstinence from or particular consumption patterns of technology. In each case, homework is crafted specifically to support the client learning more about him or her or their self based on the issues raised by the client and to discover ways in which he or she may gain conscious control and choice over behaviors through mindfully engaging the homework. Often the particulars of the assignments are not critical, but more important is the idea that clients engage the "symptoms," or their experiences, actively and mindfully. Common homework assignments include doing a particular problematic behavior more or less and seeing what arises in response. This is a typical structural intervention. Or fantasy can be helpful when people feel hopeless. Consider a client now with whom you might wish to use homework and what issues and concerns you have about doing so. Keep in mind that homework is behavioral, with the spirit of curiosity and learning through the exercises, and the goal is to encounter barriers and feelings and to deepen engagement actively. It is not assigned in order to achieve a particular end goal. Engender a sense of playfulness and allow some flexibility. Regardless of whether or not your client engages at least you can both be curious about why they are or are not willing or able to engage in their internal lives.

Rob Fisher (2002) offers an excellent framework for these kinds of homework assignments and these are often very helpful in cases of infidelity.

Exercise #10

Ask a couple to write down their fantasies about intimacy, sexuality, and connection for one another and to have them share in session. Often couples find that they cannot fully articulate a fantasy without the fear of being shut down in the presence of another. Fantasies provide keys to desire and also can provide information about the roots of the blocks to intimacy. An instance of infidelity can be a problematic way for people to address their fantasies either consciously or otherwise. Making these fantasies conscious allows for more active movement of the material within the fantasy. Often also fantasies are metaphors or narratives that can be engaged somatically, in the imaginary world, or may not need to be literal. Psychoanalysts and psychodynamically trained clinicians most certainly have a much more detailed view of how to work with fantasy material. Using these approaches to address infidelity is often very helpful albeit longer-term work.

Exercise #11

Reflecting on our technology use is important so that we might begin to facilitate such explorations for our clients. Oftentimes they are unaware of the knee-jerk emotional responses and habituated behaviors they have in their technologically mediated relationships. They receive an email and check it immediately without considering that they have a choice or not; they feel confused by someone liking their post and ascribe meaning to that but have no facial cues or other evidence to support it. Technology is not inherently bad and yet we and our clients may not know how to remain in control of the decisions we make as we engage with technology and relationships, and this can have an impact on our relationships with partners and on the ways infidelity comes to develop. It is far more powerful to teach a client through mindful technology use to be in the driver's seat than it is to suggest that the spouse monitor his or her technology devices as a way to develop trust and mitigate potential opportunities to slide into an affair again.

Reflect on your technology use and habits. How much conscious control do you have in using your tools? What happens when your phone rings, or you note that there is a text message or an email? Do you check or post on Facebook or Twitter or other social media? What happens when you do not have access to your phone or laptop or the Internet? Are there times you get comfort from people online because your actual life is challenging? Does this enhance your relationships or diminish them? Do you engage with clients via technology? What is the benefit or drawback of this? Do you say things to people via technology that you otherwise wouldn't say in person or via phone? Have you ever misinterpreted what someone typed or felt misunderstood online? Do you have emotional reactions to what others type or say via technology?

Exercise #12

Consider how much you know about porn and what your judgments are about it. Do you watch porn? If so, how much and how often? How do you decide when to watch and what to watch? Is it satisfying? What are the consequences of your porn habits on your relationship(s) and sexual life, if any? How do you feel about the bodies and sexual behavior in the porn you consume? Consider what you know about what is shown in porn you don't watch. What are your beliefs about porn consumption?[3]

Exercise #13

The notion of cultural competency and cultural humility are very helpful here and have been applied in medical practice to address the situated meanings of health and disease for diverse groups. We could just as easily apply these ideas to psychotherapy and diversity and critically question the meaning and assumptions we all bring to the issue of infidelity as well as any issue, for that matter.

In many cultures infidelity has a very different meaning. Consider your views as situated culturally and historically and personally. Consider the idea that perhaps there is nothing absolute and essential about infidelity. We live inside of cultures that interpret for us and socialize us to understand infidelity and everything else. Consider the extent that you have freedom and the extent that you are a product of time and space. In France, for example, another country that has religious freedom like the US but also is largely informed by Catholic and Protestant ideas, there is far more permission to have sex and romance outside of monogamous marriage and to flirt. What are your cultural views, and what are those of your clients? How might the meaning of affairs then be entirely different for particular cases? How much do you know about cultural norms of infidelity for the cultures from which your clients come?

Exercise #14

Consider how to build excitement, play, erotic tension, and fun into a long-term relationship. What do you imagine is required in these circumstances? What biases do you have about this issue? Do you believe, for example, that it is not possible in long-term relationships? Do you believe that only perfectly matched people can achieve this? Do you believe that we can intentionally build and tend to this? Many writers have explored this very issue, and many suggest that having curiosity for the other, sufficient individuation, and a playful attitude is helpful. How might your views on this philosophical issue inform your work with clients who are experiencing a lack of vitality or are experiencing an existential crisis?

Conclusion

The discussions and studies reported in this text suggest that infidelity is a complex experience. We do not share an agreed-upon understanding of what constitutes infidelity and it is lived in varied ways. It is also a phenomenon that is on the rise and is very common, suggesting that a moralizing and pathologizing individual focus is perhaps less relevant for the times. Our relationship to sex, marriage, divorce, and affairs is situated socio-historically and as such a renewed contemporary perspective is warranted.

Just because affairs are common and socio-historically situated, and I wish to take a descriptive curious non-pathologizing deep look into the underlying questions beneath infidelity, does not imply that I am an infidelity apologist. This book is decidedly not a book in defense of affairs, despite the fact that I suggest that affairs are lived with passive intentionality—somewhat unconsciously. I do not do so to defend the actions of those who have affairs. We are all responsible for our actions. I merely have pointed out that *within the data*, people describe a split in the layers of their consciousness between the time that precedes an affair and the actions they take in the moment. They do not seem to be aware that they are living the beginning of an affair until it is too late. They only realize this after the fact. Because there are other studies that suggest similar problems with passivity and a tendency to slide toward decisions sometimes in difficult contexts, I cannot support the idea that cheaters are bad people. My perspective, and the research supports this point, is that cheaters are people who were not aware of the dilemma they were living when it was happening. They are victims of lack of awareness and flawed perceptions. Further, our current socio-historical context is putting significant pressures on couples and these flawed perceptions are easy to embrace. Essentially, the context is ripe for us to not perceive the risk inherent in our marriages or to navigate our minds in a fully integrated and ethical manner.

Recall, what decision science research suggests, that our biased and flawed perceptions and decision-making structures make possible affairs and a great number of other similarly structured possibilities where we do something but do not correctly frame the choice as a significant risk. Evidence suggests that people behave similarly with starting smoking, for example, and fail to realize that trying one puff is a choice point after which they may slide passively toward becoming an addict without ever choosing to become an addict—they simply misperceived the meaning of the first act.

I want to further make clear that the perspective of this book is that affairs are harmful and should be avoided through awareness of the choice points that we all have in each interaction with our spouses and others every day. This is the ethical obligation we have to our spouses to choose to act in a way that is consistent with what we promised or to alter those promises through discussions before any sliding toward an affair occurs. We can only help our clients, however, if we are available to guide them to explore not only the shadow side of their marriage, but also sexuality and divorce. And to accomplish this we need not only more content knowledge but also the willingness to confront our own biases and to facilitate deeper explorations for our clients in a more balanced and open manner.

The specific content knowledge needed includes current and relevant information about sexuality (both sexual functioning and dysfunction) and problems related to Internet, technology, and porn use. Most psychotherapists lack sufficient training in sexuality, and sometimes issues that are relatively simple to address are beneath the sexual dissatisfaction that results in infidelity. It is our collective ethical obligation to develop professionally to close these knowledge gaps and attitudinal biases—not every sexual issue is rooted in the psyche. If we conceptualize every sexual issue psychodynamically and it is driven by a simple-to-solve medical issue or could be addressed easily with a short course of behavioral or sex therapy coupled with some psycho-education, perhaps we are not serving our clients' needs. It is highly recommended that all psychotherapists develop a working understanding of the various apps and tools that people use to date, hook up, and so on. It is also important that each of us continue to engage the new ideas and theories about Internet addiction, porn addiction, and sex addiction, as compared to problematic behaviors. The debates about how difficulties regulating emotions and impulses and the effects of use of the Internet, porn, video games, and apps, and how these relate to sexuality and relationships, will likely be a major focus of our times. It is important that we all participate in the dialogue and help to shape the discourse so that practice-based information and theories can converge into a professional consensus about treatment planning and directions as we move into the AI-era and continue to see more and more psychological issues that include technology.

It is my hope that these stories and their analyses in this text have been illustrative and useful and that each of you has had a chance to encounter your beliefs about infidelity and question them. I also hope you have been able to see the human side of all the scenarios in these stories and that you are able to embrace work with those who have been touched by infidelities with more depth and skill.

Notes

1 Having both individual and couples sessions concurrently represents significant financial and time investment that many people may not have the luxury of being able to afford. In cases of practical constraints, sometimes a couples therapist can accomplish some of this work through in-session work, homework

assignments, and a few strategically placed individual meetings with each to support both the system and the individual needs. This is not ideal, however, because there is a risk of triangulation, and in cases where there is significant dysregulation, separate individual sessions can be very supportive and helpful.
2 Most sex education in the US, regardless of state, lacks information on sexual pleasure, sex and aging, sex and disability, sexual practices, arousal, desire and orgasm, and other aspects of sexuality that are often important to our clients. Most formal sex education focuses on birth control, sexually transmitted infections, and reproduction. It is rare that people have adequate medically accurate, supportive, sex-positive, pleasure-positive information that is helpful in their relationships. Psychotherapists and medical professionals also have this same quandary in that they too lack knowledge on these topics, but also are tasked with treating the issues to a certain extent in their respective practices. There are a great number of workshops, books, and programs that can fill in these gaps.
3 There are a great number of websites and apps dedicated to pornography, and they target every imaginable interest and demographic group. For some porn is very helpful and useful in managing problematic sexual impulses or activities. For some porn helps them manage discrepant desire or other aspects of their partner being unavailable. Some porn stars and models find this work rewarding and empowering. Others suggest that porn causes increased sexual impulsivity, siphons off desire and energy in relationships, and inherently degrades those who engage in it. All of these views can be supported through research, case study, or theories. The wise clinician can make space for any of these to be possible in assessing and treating clinical cases that involve porn use. The critical questions to consider are the consequences of the porn use, the degree to which the participant feels he or she or they can choose, and the distress experienced as a result. The meanings that each client has attached to porn are important considerations as well.

Reference

Fisher, R. (2002). *Experiential Psychotherapy with Couples: A Guide for the Creative Pragmatist*. New York, NY: Zeig, Tucker & Theisen.

Bibliography

Allen, E., & Atkins, D. (2012). The association of divorce and extramarital sex in a representative US sample. *Journal of Family Issues*, 33(11), p. 1477.

American Psychiatric Association. (1952). *Diagnostic and Statistical Manual—1st edition*. Washington, DC: APA.

American Psychiatric Association. (2013). *Diagnostic and Statistical Manual—5th edition*. Washington, DC: APA.

Aponte, H. (1985). The negotiation of values in therapy. *Family Process*, 24(3), p. 323.

Asexuality Visibility Education Network (AVEN). (2017). Retrieved from: www.asexuality.org.

Atkins, D., Baucom, D., & Jacobson, N. (2001). Understanding infidelity: Correlates in a national random sample. *Journal of Family Psychology*, 15(4), p. 735.

Barta, W., & Kiene, S. (2005). Motivations for infidelity in heterosexual dating couples: The roles of gender, personality differences and socio-sexual orientation. *Journal of Social and Personal Relationships*, 22(3), p. 339.

Beard, K. W. (2002). Internet addiction: Current status and implications for employees. *Journal of Employment Counseling*, 39, 2–11.

Bettinger, M. (2005). A family systems approach to working with sexually open gay male couples. *Journal of Couple and Relationship Therapy*, 4(2/3), p. 149.

Bordin, E. (1979). The generalizability of the psychoanalytic concept of the working alliance. *Psychotherapy: Theory, Research and Practice*, 16(3), pp. 252–260.

Braun-Harvey, M., & Vigorito, M. (2016). *Treating Out of Control Sexual Behavior: Rethinking Sex Addiction*. New York, NY: Springer.

Brown, E. (2005). Split self affairs and their treatment. *Journal of Couple and Relationship Therapy*, 4(2/3), p. 55.

Campbell, B., & Wright, D. (2010). Marriage today: Exploring the incongruence between American's beliefs and practices. *Journal of Comparative Family Studies*, 41(3), p. 329.

Case, B. (2005). Healing the wounds of infidelity through the healing power of apology and forgiveness. *Journal of Couple and Relationship Therapy*, 4(2/3), p. 41.

Catania, J., Gibson, D., Marin, B., Coates, T., & Greenblatt, R. (1990). Response bias in assessing sexual behaviors relevant to HIV transmission. *Evaluation and Program Planning*, 13(1), p. 19.

Coontz, S. (2006). *Marriage, A History: How Love Conquered Marriage.* New York, NY: Penguin Group.

Cossman, B. (2006). The new politics of adultery. *Columbia Journal of Gender and Law,* 15(1), p. 274.

Cott, N. (2000). *Public Vows: A History of Marriage and the Nation.* Cambridge, MA: Harvard University Press.

DeStefano, J., & Oala, M. (2008). Extramarital affairs: Basic considerations and essential tasks in clinical work. *The Family Journal,* 16(1), p. 13.

Douthat, R. (2008). Is pornography adultery? *Atlantic Monthly,* 302(3), p. 80.

Drigotas, S., & Barta, W. (2001). The cheating heart: Scientific explorations of infidelity. *Current Directions in Psychological Science,* 10(5), p. 177.

Duba, J., Kindsvatter, A., & Lara, T. (2008). Treating infidelity: Considering narratives of attachment. *Family Journal,* 16(4), p. 293.

Dunn, M., Martin, N., Bailey, J., Heath, A., Bucholz, K., Madden, P., & Statham, D. (1997). Participation bias in a sexuality survey: Psychological and behavioral characteristics of responders and nonresponders. *International Journal of Epidemiology,* 26(4), p. 844.

Dupree, J., White, M., Charlotte, O., & Lafleur, C. (2007). Infidelity treatment patterns: A practice-based evidence approach. *The American Journal of Family Therapy,* 35(4), p. 327.

Eagleton, T. (1983). *Literary Theory: An Introduction.* Oxford: Basil Blackwell.

Easton, D., & Hardy, J. (2009). *The Ethical Slut: A Practical Guide to Polyamory, Open Relationships and Other Adventures.* Berkeley, CA: Celestial Arts.

Eaves, S., & Robertson-Smith, M. (2007). The relationship between self-worth and marital infidelity: A pilot study. *The Family Journal,* 15(4), p. 382.

Englander, M. (2012). The interview: Data collection in descriptive phenomenological human scientific research. *Journal of Phenomenological Psychology,* 43(1), p. 13.

Farkas, G., Sine, L., & Evans, I. (1978). Personality, sexuality and demographic differences between volunteers and nonvolunteers for a laboratory study of male behavior. *Archives of Sexual Behavior,* 7, p. 513.

Fenton, K., Johnson, A., McManus, S., & Erens, B. (2001). Measuring sexual behavior: Methodological challenges in survey research. *Sexually Transmitted Infections,* 77(2), pp. 84–92.

Fife, S., Weeks, G., & Stellberg-Filbert, J. (2013). Facilitating forgiveness in the treatment of infidelity: An interpersonal model. *Journal of Family,* 35(4), p. 343.

Fisher, R. (2002). *Experiential Psychotherapy with Couples: A Guide for the Creative Pragmatist.* New York, NY: Zeig, Tucker & Theisen.

Foucault, M. (1990). *The History of Sexuality: An Introduction.* New York, NY: Random House.

Fouche, F. (1993). Phenomenological theory of human science. In Snyman, J. (Ed.), *Conceptions of Social Inquiry* (pp. 87–112). Pretoria, South Africa: Human Science Research Council.

Gilovich, T., Griffen, D., & Kahneman, D. (2002). *Heuristics and Biases: The Psychology of Intuitive Judgment.* New York, NY: Cambridge University Press.

Giorgi, A. (2009). *The Descriptive Phenomenological Method in Psychology: A Modified Husserlian Approach.* Pittsburgh, PA: Duquesne University Press.

Glass, S. (2003). *Not "Just Friends": Rebuilding Trust and Recovering Your Sanity After Infidelity*. New York, NY: Simon & Schuster.

Groenewald, T. (2004). A phenomenological research design illustrated. *International Journal of Qualitative Methods*, 3(1), p. 1.

Hall, J., & Fincham, F. (2009). Psychological distress: Precursor or consequence of dating infidelity? *Personality and Social Psychology Bulletin*, 35(2), p. 143.

Halling, S. (2008). *Intimacy, Transcendence and Psychology*. New York, NY: Palgrave Macmillan.

Hertlein, K., & Piercy, F. (2008). Therapists' assessment and treatment of Internet infidelity cases. *Journal of Marriage and Family Therapy*, 34(4), p. 481.

Hertlein, K., & Piercy, F. (2012). Essential elements of Internet infidelity treatment. *Journal of Marriage and Family Therapy*, 38(S1), p. 257.

Hertlein, K., Piercy, F., & Wetchler, J. (2005). *Handbook of the Clinical Treatment of Infidelity*. New York, NY: Haworth Press.

Horvath, A. (2005). The therapeutic relationship: Research and theory. *Psychotherapy Research*, 15(1–2).

Horvath, A., & Greenberg, L. (2005). *The Working Alliance: Theory, Research and Practice*. San Francisco, CA: Wiley Publishers.

Horvath, A., & Symonds, D. (1991). Relation between working alliance and outcome in psychotherapy: A meta-analysis. *Journal of Counseling Psychology*, 38(2), p. 139–149.

Hurlbert, D. (1992). Factors influencing a woman's decision to end an extramarital sexual relationship. *Journal of Sex and Marital Therapy*, 18(2), p. 104.

Husserl, E. (1913/1982). *Ideas Pertaining to a Pure Phenomenology and to a Phenomenological Philosophy: First Book*. Norwell, MA: Kluwer Academic Publishers.

Husserl, E. (1900/2001). *Logical Investigations*, Ed. Dermot Moran. 2nd ed. 2 vols. London, UK: Routledge.

Jacobson, L., & Mather, M. (2011). A post recession update on US social and economic trends. *Population Reference Bureau*. Retrieved from: www.prb.org/Publications/Reports/2011/us-economicsocialtrends-update2.aspx

Jeanfreau, M., Jurich, A., & Mong, M. (2014). Risk factors associated with women's marital infidelity. *Contemporary Family Therapy*, 36(1), p. 327.

Johnson, S. (2005). *The Practice of Emotionally Focused Couple Therapy: Creating Connection*. New York, NY: Brunner-Routledge.

Kahneman, D. (2012). *Thinking Fast and Slow*. New York, NY: Farrar, Strauss and Giroux.

Kleese, C. (2014). Polyamory: Intimate practice, identity or sexual orientation. *Sexualities*, 17(1/2), p. 81.

Kruger, J., Burrus, J., & Kressel, L. (2009). Between a rock and a hard place: Dammed if you do, dammed if you don't. *Journal of Experimental Social Psychology*, 45(6), p. 1286.

Lammers, J., Stoker, J., Jordan, J., Pollman, M., & Stapel, D. (2011). Power increases infidelity among men and woman. *Psychological Science*, 22(9), p. 1191.

Linehan, M. (1993). *Cognitive-Behavioral Treatment of Borderline Personality Disorder*. New York, NY: Guillford Press.

Lusterman, D. (2005a). Helping children and adults cope with parental infidelity. *Journal of Clinical Psychology*, 61(11), p. 1439.

Lusterman, D. (2005b). Marital infidelity: The effects of delayed traumatic reaction. *Journal of Couple and Relationship Therapy*, 4(2/3), p. 71.

Marcus, B., & Schütz, A. (2005). Who are the people reluctant to participate in research? Personality correlates of four different types of nonresponse as inferred from self-and observer ratings. *Journal of Personality*, 73(4), p. 959.

McNulty, J. (2013). The implication of sexual narcissism for sexual and marital satisfaction. *Archives of Sexual Behavior*, 42(6), p. 1021.

Merleau-Ponty, M. (2012/1945). *Phenomenology of Perception*. New York, NY: Routledge.

Meston, C., Heiman, J., Trapnell, P., & Paulhus, D. (1998). Socially desirable responding and sexuality self-reports. *Journal of Sex Research*, 35(2), p. 148.

Morin, J. (1996). *The Erotic Mind*. New York, NY: Harper Perennial.

Nelson, T., Piercy, F., & Sprenkle, D. (2005). Internet infidelity: A multi-phase Delphi study. *Journal of Couple and Relationship Therapy*, 4(2/3), p. 173.

Owen, J., Rhoades, G., & Stanley, S. (2013). Sliding versus deciding in relationships: Associations with relationship quality, commitment and infidelity. *Journal of Couples and Relationship Therapy*, 12(2), pp. 135–149.

Perel, E. (2007). *Mating in Captivity: Unlocking Erotic Intelligence*. New York, NY: Harper Collins.

Pittman, F., & Wagers, T. (2005). The relationship, if any between marriage and infidelity. *Journal of Couple and Relationship Therapy*, 4(2/3), p. 103.

Plaud, J., Gaither, G., Hegsted, H., Rowan, L., & Devitt, M. (1999). Volunteer bias in human psychophysiological sexual arousal research: To whom do our research results apply? *The Journal of Sex Research*, 36(2).

Ryan, C., & Jetha, C. (2011). *Sex at Dawn: How We Mate, Why We Stray, and What It Means for Modern Relationships*. New York, NY: Harper Collins.

Safran, J., & Muran, C. (2000). *Negotiating the Therapeutic Alliance: A Relational Treatment Guide*. New York, NY: Guilford Press.

Schnarch, D. (2009). *Passionate Marriage: Keeping Love and Intimacy Alive in Committed Relationships*. New York, NY: Norton and Co.

Schorn, T. (2017). *Blogpost: Chump Lady*. Retrieved from: www.chumplady.com

Seidman, I. (1998). *Interviewing as Qualitative Research*. New York, NY: Teachers College Press.

Slovic, P. (2000). *The Perception of Risk*. New York, NY: Earthscan.

Snyder, D., Balderrama-Durbin, C., & Fissette, C. (2012). Treating infidelity and comorbid depression: A case study involving military deployment. *Couple and Family Psychology: Research and Practice*, 1(3), p. 213.

Stalfa, F., & Hastings, C. (2005). "Accusatory Suffering" in the offended spouse. *Journal of Couple and Relationship Therapy*, 4(2/3), p. 83.

Sterba, R. (1934). The fate of the ego in analytic therapy. *International Journal of Psycho-Analysis*, 42(3), p. 117.

Welman, J., & Kruger, S. (1999). *Research Methodology for the Business and Administrative Sciences*. Johannesburg, South Africa: International Thompson.

Whitty, M., & Carr, A. (2005). Taking the good with the bad: Applying Klein's work to further our understandings of cyber-cheating. *Journal of Couple and Relationship Therapy*, 4(2/3), p. 103.

Widman, L., & McNulty, J. (2014). Sexual narcissism and infidelity in early marriage. *Archives of Sexual Behavior*, 43(7), pp. 1315–1325.

Young, K. (2008). Internet sex addiction: Risk factors, stages of development and treatment. *American Behavioral Scientist*, 52(1), p. 21.

Zapien, N. (2016). The beginning of an extra-marital affair: A phenomenological study and clinical implications. *Journal of Phenomenological Psychology*, 47(2), p. 134.

Index

abortions 5, 14n4
abuse: domestic violence and 44; intimate partner violence (IPV) 34, 97, 102; sexual 42, 79, 108, 121; substance 23
ADHD 23, 102
adultery 4–5, 14n6, 20
affair: aftermath of 34; constituents of infidelity 75–89; essential structure of beginning of infidelity 73–75; infidelity in form of 19–20; recognition of 85–87; reflection and bracketing by therapists 53–59; research of 22–23; term 4; views of professionals on 23; *see also* infidelity structure
affair narratives 61; case of Tammy and Larry 134–141; describing view of self and partner 81–82; man considering affair stabilizing his marriage 71–73; participant describing role of technology in 62–66; woman's description of affair 68–71; woman's sexual relationship not considered an "affair" 66–68
affair not recognized until after it begins: clinical treatment directions for 128–129; constituents of infidelity 85–87
American Association of Sex Educators, Counselors, and Therapists (AASECT) 54, 145
Asexuality Visibility Education Network (AVEN) 43
attachment theory, sexuality 35
Autism Spectrum Disorder 102

BDSM 100
betrayal 4, 5; perception of 5–7, 9; types of 4, 14n2
biases of therapists 32–33, 44, 93, 129–130
bipolar disorder 102
birth control 4–5
bisexual 34
Borderline Personality Disorder 127

California Institute of Integral Studies 11
case example (Tammy and Larry) 134–141
child custody 5, 22
clinical treatment directions 93–95; for affair not recognized until after it begins 128–129; alignment of goals for 95–101; assessment of infidelity cases 101–104; for dissatisfaction and hopeless in relationships 106–115; when divorce or opening up relationship not considered real options 129–132; for experience of desire and passion overriding/overtaking judgment 127–128; intimacy 94–95; for lack of curiosity for partner as subject 125–126; for partner and the self viewed as fixed characters 122–125; problematic perceptions making affairs possible 104–106; for sense of deserving sexual satisfaction/intimate connection 120–122; for value of novelty and passion in romantic/ sexual relationships 116–120

3–4; *see also* clinical treatment
directions
infidelity structure: constituents
of 76; desire overtaking and
overriding one's judgment 83–85;
dissatisfaction and hopelessness
in relationship 76–78; explication
of constituents 75–89; lacking
curiosity for partner as subject
82–83; not recognizing divorce
or opening up relationship as real
options 87–89; recognizing affair
only after it begins 85–87; sense
of deserving sexual satisfaction or
intimate connection 79–80; value
of novelty and passion in romantic/
sexual relationships 78–79; viewing
partner and self as fixed characters
80–82
Instagram 37, 38
Institutional Review Board (IRB)
11, 51
intentionality 7, 13, 48, 85, 87, 158
Internet addiction/use 23; client
reporting Internet addiction
99–100; exercise 152; research of
24–25, 27n2
intimacy 8, 34, 38, 40–41, 88:
authenticity and 94–95; as
connection 94, 104, 107;
description of 94; fear of 115;
infidelity and lacking 73–74, 77,
79; narratives discussing 40–41, 65,
68, 70
intimate partner violence (IPV) 34,
97, 102

Johnson, Sue 35

lack of curiosity for partner as subject:
clinical treatment directions for
125–126; constituent of infidelity
82–83
lesbian couple, sex as focus of
treatment 40–42
LGBT Americans 24, 51, 54
LinkedIn 37, 38

marriage: data from U.S. Census
Bureau 23–24; exercises 142,
154; financial and legal contract
5; narrative describing affair as
stabilizing 71–73; protecting

from outside threats 34; research
of marital dissatisfaction 21–22;
revisionist wedding vows 24
Mating in Captivity (Perel) 35
mental health 22, 33, 39

narcissism: entitlement and 121–122;
narcissistic personality disorder 31,
102, 121–122
nature versus nurture 21, 132n2
no-fault divorce laws 5
nymphomaniacs 20, 27n1

OCD (obsessive-compulsive disorder)
102
open relationships 4, 49, 51, 58, 93,
142; difficulty of 88; example of
solution for infidelity 130–131;
feelings about 43; managing
differences 42; research 23–24;
separating sex and love 81; variety
in 38–39
Obergefell v. Hodges (2015) 24, 28n3

pansexual 34
participant recruitment,
phenomenological research method
49–51
partner and the self viewed as fixed
characters: clinical treatment
directions for 122–125; constituent
of infidelity 80–82
perceptions: of betrayals 14n6, 21;
bracketing, by therapists 53–59;
description of 47–48; flawed
156; of infidelity 5–7, 9, 12;
interventions for shifting 109–111;
of partner and the self 80–82,
122–125; series of, co-occurring
before infidelity 104–106; sex
and monogamy 23–24; *see also*
infidelity structure
Perel, Esther 35
phenomenological research methods
47–49; collecting narratives
51–52; Giorgi's, for psychology
48–49, 52–53, 59–60; perceptions
that co-occur with infidelity 105;
recruiting participants 49–51;
reflection and bracketing by
researchers 53–59; *see also* affair
narratives; clinical treatment
directions